Geomancy and Ancient Astrology

A Guide to Earth Divination, the Zodiac Signs, and Astrological Wisdom from the Babylonians, Egyptians, and Greeks

© Copyright 2023 - All rights reserved.

The content contained within this book may not be reproduced, duplicated, or transmitted without direct written permission from the author or the publisher.

Under no circumstances will any blame or legal responsibility be held against the publisher, or author, for any damages, reparation, or monetary loss due to the information contained within this book, either directly or indirectly.

Legal Notice:

This book is copyright protected. It is only for personal use. You cannot amend, distribute, sell, use, quote, or paraphrase any part, or the content within this book, without the consent of the author or publisher.

Disclaimer Notice:

Please note the information contained within this document is for educational and entertainment purposes only. All effort has been executed to present accurate, up-to-date, reliable, and complete information. No warranties of any kind are declared or implied. Readers acknowledge that the author is not engaging in the rendering of legal, financial, medical, or professional advice. The content within this book has been derived from various sources. Please consult a licensed professional before attempting any techniques outlined in this book.

By reading this document, the reader agrees that under no circumstances is the author responsible for any losses, direct or indirect, that are incurred as a result of the use of the information contained within this document, including, but not limited to, errors, omissions, or inaccuracies.

Your Free Gift
(only available for a limited time)

Thanks for getting this book! If you want to learn more about various spirituality topics, then join Mari Silva's community and get a free guided meditation MP3 for awakening your third eye. This guided meditation mp3 is designed to open and strengthen ones third eye so you can experience a higher state of consciousness. Simply visit the link below the image to get started.

https://spiritualityspot.com/meditation

Table of Contents

PART 1: GEOMANCY 1
   INTRODUCTION 2
   CHAPTER 1: INTRODUCTION TO GEOMANCY 4
   CHAPTER 2: WHY PLANETS MATTER 14
   CHAPTER 3: THE ELEMENTS AND THE ZODIAC SIGNS 28
   CHAPTER 4: THE GEOMANTIC HOUSES 38
   CHAPTER 5: PREPARING YOUR MIND 47
   CHAPTER 6: CASTING THE POINTS 56
   CHAPTER 7: THE GEOMANTIC FIGURES 66
   CHAPTER 8: CONSTRUCTING A SHIELD CHART 87
   CHAPTER 9: GENERATING AN ASTROLOGICAL CHART 95
   CHAPTER 10: METHODS OF INTERPRETATION 104
   CONCLUSION 110
PART 2: ANCIENT ASTROLOGY 112
   INTRODUCTION 113
   CHAPTER 1: INTRODUCTION TO ANCIENT ASTROLOGY 115
   CHAPTER 2: THE FIVE WANDERING STARS AND THE TWO LIGHTS 123
   CHAPTER 3: BABYLON: WHERE ASTROLOGY WAS BORN 132
   CHAPTER 4: EGYPTIAN ASTROLOGY AND THE DECANS 140
   CHAPTER 5: THE EGYPTIAN ZODIAC SIGNS 150
   CHAPTER 6: HELLENISTIC ASTROLOGY I. THE TOPOI 167
   CHAPTER 7: HELLENISTIC ASTROLOGY II. THE ZOIDIA 175

CHAPTER 8: THE THEMA MUNDI AND HELLENISTIC CHARTS..........183
CHAPTER 9: THE HERMETIC LOTS..190
CHAPTER 10: ANCIENT HELLENISTIC TECHNIQUES 197
CHAPTER 11: MAKE YOUR OWN ASTROLABE..203
CONCLUSION..207
BONUS: GLOSSARY OF ASTROLOGICAL TERMS....................................209
HERE'S ANOTHER BOOK BY MARI SILVA THAT YOU MIGHT LIKE 214
YOUR FREE GIFT (ONLY AVAILABLE FOR A LIMITED TIME)...................215

Part 1: Geomancy

Unlocking the Magic of Earth Divination for Beginners

Introduction

"The five elements are energies, not things. In Hinduism, they are known as the five tattvas. Psychic people can see them and their geometric forms."

~~Stefan Emunds

Have you ever wondered what your future holds? Have you ever looked up at the stars and felt a deep connection to the cosmos? If so, you may be interested in learning about geomancy.

Geomancy is an ancient form of divination that uses the power of the earth to answer your questions. It is a form of earth magic that can be used to gain insight into your past, present, and future. The word "geomancy" comes from the Greek words geo (earth) and manteia (divination). The word "geomancy" can also be used to refer to the study of the earth's energy field.

Geomancy has been around for centuries and is still used today. There is no perfect way to do it because each practitioner has their techniques and preferences. However, the basic premise is that we can gain insights into our lives and the future by using the natural world as a mirror. This guide will teach you the basics of geomancy, including how to cast your geomantic chart.

In the first chapter, we will explore the history and origins of geomancy. We will also discuss the elements that form the basis of this practice. In the second chapter, we will discuss why planets matter in geomancy. We will look at the zodiac signs in the third chapter and how they connect to the elements. The fourth chapter will focus on the geomantic houses and their meanings.

In the fifth chapter, we will discuss how to prepare your mind for a geomantic reading. The sixth chapter will teach you how to cast geomantic points. The seventh chapter will focus on the different geomantic figures and their meanings. We will show you how to construct a shield chart in the eighth chapter. The ninth chapter will focus on generating an astrological chart. Finally, in the tenth chapter, we will discuss different methods of interpretation.

You will also find a bonus section with printables to help you start your geomancy practice. With the help of this easy-to-understand guide, you will be able to tap into the power of the earth and use it to gain insights into your life and your future. So, regardless of whether you are a beginner or an experienced practitioner, this guide will provide you with everything you need to know about geomancy. So, let us get started!

Chapter 1: Introduction to Geomancy

Are you looking for a way to understand yourself and your place in the universe? Do you want to know what your destiny holds? Geomancy can help you get answers to these questions and more.

Geomancy is rooted in nature.
https://pixabay.com/es/photos/avenida-%c3%a1rboles-sendero-815297/

Many considered a divination system as old as time; geomancy was once practiced by cultures all around the world. This system of divination implied direct contact with the earth, the spirit realm, and astrological alignments. In this chapter, we will look at geomancy's interesting cultural and historical background. We will also explore how to practice this ancient type of divination.

Geomancy - The Divination System

Geomancy is a divination system that uses the earth to understand the hidden forces at work in our lives. Also known as "earth magic," geomancy is rooted in the belief that the land is alive and has wisdom to share with us. The word "geomancy" comes from the Greek geo (earth) and manteia (divination).

To practice geomancy, one simply needs to spend time in nature and attune oneself to the earth's subtle energies. The shapes and patterns of the land can then be interpreted as clues to our highest potential and deepest desires. By connecting with the earth through geomancy, we can access our hidden power and learn to live in harmony with the natural world.

A Brief History

Geomancy is an ancient practice that has its roots in the shamanic traditions of Africa, Asia, and the Americas. It is also one of the oldest forms of divination in Europe, where the Celts and other indigenous peoples used it.

Geomancy uses the placement of objects to interpret the will of the universe. The word "geomancy" comes from the Greek word for earth, and it is thought that the first geomancers were likely priests or shamans who used rocks, sticks, and dirt to divine the future.

The first written record of geomancy comes from ancient India, where it was known as "Vastu Shastra." This Hindu text describes the use of geomancy to find the perfect location for a home or temple. In China, geomancy was known as "Feng Shui," and it was used to align buildings and burial sites with the flow of "chi," or life force energy.

In Europe, Geomancy was used by the Celts and other indigenous peoples to find sacred sites for their tribes. The Druids, in particular, were known for their skill in reading the land. They would often travel to far-flung places in search of special places to build their temples and altars.

During the Middle Ages, geomancy was popular among both Christians and Muslims. It was also used by the Knights Templar, who were said to have used geomantic symbols in their magical rituals. The Renaissance saw a revival of interest in geomancy, as many scholars began to rediscover the ancient texts that described this divination system.

Over time, the practice of Geomancy spread to other cultures, and different methods of divination developed. In Europe, for example, geomancers began using bags of sand or dirt to create patterns that could be interpreted. Today, there are many different schools of geomancy, each with its methods and traditions. Although some people may view it as a superstitious practice, geomancy has been used for centuries to help people make important decisions about their lives.

Cultural Relevance

Geomancy has played an important role in many cultures around the world. In Africa, it is still used by traditional healers and shamans to diagnose and treat illness. In Asia, it is used to select auspicious locations for homes and businesses. And in the Americas, Native American tribes have used geomancy for everything from choosing hunting grounds to predicting the future.

Although it is not as well-known as other divination systems like tarot reading or astrology, geomancy is still practiced by people all over the world. And with its simple techniques and earth-based approach, geomancy is a great way to connect with the natural world and access our hidden power.

Geomancy is a very practical method of finding answers to specific questions. It involves interpreting patterns in the earth to gain insight into a particular issue, for example, the placement of rocks or the shape of a mountain. This might seem like an arcane or outdated practice, but it is quite useful in modern times. For example, geomancers have been used to help locate natural resources, assess environmental impact, and predict natural disasters.

In addition, the principles of geomancy can be applied to more everyday matters, such as choosing a location for a new home or business. Whether you are looking for answers on a global or personal scale, geomancy is worth considering. The next time you have a question, why not ask the earth?

The Practice of Geomancy

Traditionally, geomancers would use sticks, stones, or other objects to create patterns in the dirt. These patterns would then be interpreted according to a set of rules to divine information about the future or answer specific questions. Although the practice of geomancy has largely been forgotten in the modern world, it remains an interesting way to engage with the natural world and gain insight into the hidden forces at play in our lives.

Geomancy is a simple and accessible way to connect with the earth and receive guidance from the natural world. All you need is a piece of paper, a pencil, or a bag of sand or dirt. To begin, you will need to clear your mind and focus on your question. Once you are ready, start making marks on the paper or in the sand. There is no right or wrong way to do this, just allow your hand to move freely.

After making a few marks, take a step back and examine the patterns you have made. See if you can find any shapes or symbols that seem to stand out. Once you have found a few potential symbols, look up their meanings in a geomancy guidebook or online. With a little practice, the accuracy of your readings may surprise you!

The Different Types of Geomancy

There are several different types of geomancy, but they all use the same basic principles, the belief that everything on Earth is connected to the universe above it and that everything has its unique energy pattern. Astrologers have long believed that each planet influences a specific part of our lives and personalities. Therefore, they believe that by studying these patterns, they can predict events or outcomes in your life.

Elemental Geomancy

The most common type of geomancy is called elemental geomancy. Simply put, it is the practice of using the elements of earth, air, fire, and water to create harmony in our lives. This may sound like a new age concept, but the truth is that people have been using these principles for centuries. For example, Feng Shui is a form of elemental geomancy that has been used in China for millennia. The basic idea is that by aligning our environment with the natural flow of energy, we can create balance and harmony in our lives.

There are many different ways to practice elemental geomancy. One popular method is to use crystals and stones to create an energetically balanced space. Placing these stones in specific areas can help redirect energy flow and create a more positive environment. Another way to harness the power of the elements is through meditation and visualization. We can access their wisdom and guidance by connecting with the elementals, the spirits of earth, air, fire, and water.

The method also involves interpreting patterns made by dividing a map into four quadrants, each representing one of the four elements, air, fire, water, and earth. There are many different methods of dividing up the map and reading the results, but all involve finding a balance between opposing elements within each quadrant.

Whether you want to create more balance in your life or simply connect with nature on a deeper level, elemental geomancy may be worth exploring. You may be surprised at how helpful and accurate this ancient practice can be with a little practice.

Astrological Geomancy

Astrological Geomancy is also known as Astronomical Geomancy and was one of the earliest forms of geomancy developed by ancient civilizations in Babylon, Egypt, and Greece. In this type of geomancy, a chart is created that shows the movement of celestial bodies in relation to each other at a given time and place. The chart is then used to determine what the future holds for an individual based on their birth date or time of birth.

Astrological geomancy uses constellations and other astronomical phenomena instead of elements on a map to generate predictions about future events. The most common version involves interpreting how specific constellations will look at sunrise in your location on a particular day to determine what will happen in your life over the next week, month, or year.

This type of geomancy was practiced in Europe until about 1550, when Pope Paul III prohibited it due to its association with magic and witchcraft. Today, there is a resurgence of interest in astrological Geomancy, and many modern practitioners believe that it can be used to gain insight into our lives, relationships, and career choices.

Many resources are available online and in libraries, if you are interested in exploring astrological geomancy. Start by finding a birth chart calculator so you can create your chart. Once you have your chart, take time to research the different placements and what they mean. The more you know about astrological geomancy, the more accurate your readings will be.

Numerological Geomancy

Numerology is the study of numbers and their influence on our lives. Each number has its energy and vibration that can impact our thoughts, feelings, and actions. Numerological Geomancy is the practice of using numbers to understand our lives and make predictions.

There are many different ways to calculate your numbers, but the most common method is to use your birth date. Once you have your numbers, you can start to interpret their meaning. Each number has a range of qualities associated with it, so you can use this information to gain insight into your personality, strengths, and challenges.

Numerological geomancy can be used for various purposes, such as understanding your relationships, making career choices, or predicting the future. You can find more information about this type of geomancy by doing an online search or visiting your local bookstores and libraries. Start by calculating your numbers, and then take some time to research their meanings.

Spiritual Geomancy

Few people know about spiritual geomancy, but it is a fascinating subject. It is the practice of using the earth's energy to heal and balance the mind, body, and spirit. Spiritual geomancy takes this one step further by using the earth's energy to connect with the spiritual realm. This can be done in many ways, but some of the most popular methods include meditating in nature, using crystals and stones, and working with plant spirits.

This type of geomancy is used to communicate with spirits and angels. The practitioner draws a mandala on the ground, representing the universe and its spiritual energy. The person then draws lines between each planet in the solar system and meditates on their questions before drawing them on paper or parchment. This type of geomancy can be used for a variety of purposes, such as guidance, protection, and healing.

Spiritual geomancy is based on astrology but focuses more on spiritual influences than physical ones. Spiritual geomancy uses astrological charts to determine how certain planets influence your life. It also looks at things like your birth date and time, and your name.

Like the other types, you'll find plenty of resources online or in libraries/book stores should you wish to learn more about spiritual geomancy. Start by finding a mandala or other symbol that resonates with you, and then take some time to research the different meanings. You may also want to find a quiet place in nature where you can meditate and connect with the earth's energy.

There are many different types of geomancy, each with its unique history and practice. The three most popular types of geomancy are astrological, numerological, and spiritual. Astrological geomancy is the practice of using the positions of celestial bodies to understand our lives. Numerological geomancy is the practice of using numbers to understand our lives. Spiritual geomancy is the practice of using the earth's energy to connect with the spiritual realm.

Geomantic Figures

Geomantic figures are shapes that are used in divination. A total of 16 figures were created by combining pairs of dots in various ways. Each figure has its meaning which can be interpreted according to the question at hand. For example, the figure known as "Populus" is typically associated with emotional turmoil, while "Acquisitio" represents gain and abundance.

The 16 geomantic figures.
https://commons.wikimedia.org/wiki/File:Geomantic_figures.svg

Geomantic figures are made up of four parts:
1. **The Natal Square:** The natal square is the most important part of any reading. It shows how all the lines interact with each other and what they mean together.
2. **The Line:** Each line represents one path that your life can take. It may be positive or negative, but it will always affect your success, happiness, and overall well-being.
3. **The House:** Each house represents a different area of life. Some houses affect your career; others affect your love life, and so on. Each house has its meaning and its own set of rules that must be followed when interpreting it correctly.
4. **The Element:** This element indicates how strongly each house affects you. If it is in detriment, this particular house will have little impact on your life, but if it is prominent, this house will have a huge impact on you.

Creating Geomantic Figures

There are many ways to create geomantic figures, but the most common method is dividing a square or circle into four equal parts. This can be done with a pencil and paper or by using a compass. Once the square or circle has been divided, the resulting quadrants can be subdivided similarly. This process is continued until there are 16 small squares or circles. These 16 figures are then interpreted according to their position within the overall design.

You will need a piece of paper and a pen to create a geomantic figure. Begin by drawing four lines of dots, making sure that each line contains an equal number of dots. Then, connect the dots in pairs to create the eight basic figures. Once you have the basic figures, you can combine them to create the other eight figures. Finally, you will need to interpret the meaning of each figure according to its position within the design.

Geomancy can be an enjoyable and rewarding activity for people of all ages. It can also be used as a tool for self-reflection and personal growth. If you are interested in exploring geomancy further, there are many resources available online and in libraries. Start by finding a mandala or other symbol that resonates with you, and then take some time to research the different meanings.

Interpreting Geomantic Figures

Geomantic figures can be used for divination to find hidden treasures or simply to admire the beauty of the earth's patterns. One must first understand the basics of line and form to interpret a geomantic figure. The most basic element of a geomantic figure is the line. Lines can be either straight or curved, and they can intersect or run parallel to one another.

The second basic element is formation; these can be either organic or geometric. Organic forms occur naturally, such as mountains, trees, and rivers; geometric forms are man-made, such as buildings, roads, and bridges. By studying the lines and forms of a geomantic figure, one can begin to see the hidden meaning within.

To interpret a geomantic figure, simply look up the meaning of the individual components and then piece together an answer to your question. With a little practice, you will be able to read geomantic figures with ease.

Geomancy in Practice

Geomancy is one of many forms of divination that uses a method called "reading the signs." It means interpreting patterns in the natural world around us. Geomancy can be done in any location, at any time, but it is best done outdoors. For this reason, it is often done at sunrise or sunset when light and shadows are most clear.

Although it may seem complicated at first, geomancy is quite simple. With a little practice, anyone can learn to read the signs of the earth.

There are two basic steps to geomancy, creating the figures and interpreting them. To create the figures, you will need a piece of paper and something to draw with. Begin by drawing 16 small squares in a 4×4 grid. Once the squares are drawn, randomly fill each square with one or two dots. This will create a figure known as a "mother."

Next, draw a line down the center of each column and row, splitting the mother into 16 smaller squares, or "daughters." Finally, count the dots in each daughter square and draw a line to connect any two squares that have the same number of dots. This will create your geomantic figure.

To interpret the figure, begin by looking at the overall shape. Is it curved or straight? Is it symmetrical or asymmetrical? Each type of shape corresponds to a different element, earth, air, fire, or water, and can provide clues about your question.

Next, look at the individual lines and forms within the figure. What do they remind you of? Do they create any patterns? Each line and form has a different meaning, so take some time to look up the symbolism associated with each one.

Finally, consider the position of the figure within the design. Is it in the center or off to the side? Is it above or below the other figures? The position of a particular figure can provide clues about the timing of an event or the importance of a question.

Geomancy is an ancient practice that involves using patterns in the earth to gain insights into the future. Geomancers believe that the earth is alive and full of energy and that by reading its patterns, we can tap into its unlimited knowledge. By interpreting the stick's movement, the geomancer can gain insights into the future. Another popular method is to read the patterns formed by stones or leaves.

By studying the shapes and colors of these patterns, the geomancer can glean information about what is to come. Regardless of which method you use, geomancy can be a powerful tool to gain insight into the future.

Geomancy is a fascinating way to study the earth and its hidden meanings. Practiced by cultures worldwide, it is a great way to connect with the natural world. By understanding the basics of line and form, you can begin to interpret the hidden messages in the earth's patterns. With a little practice, anyone can learn to read the signs of the earth!

Chapter 2: Why Planets Matter

Are you curious about how the planets influence your day-to-day life? Do you want to know more about the connection between astrology and geomancy?

Astrology is the study of the movements and relative positions of celestial bodies interpreted as having an influence on human affairs and the natural world. Geomancy, on the other hand, is a form of divination that interprets markings on the earth, either in the sand or soil, to answer questions about the future. This chapter will explore the connection between these two ancient practices.

Astrology and geomancy go hand in hand.
https://pixabay.com/es/photos/sistema-solar-sol-mercurio-venus-439046/

We will explore the role of planets in geomancy and show you how to use astrology to interpret your geomantic readings. We will start with a brief overview of the importance of planets in geomancy, followed by an exploration of each planet and how its energy manifests.

Importance of Planets in Geomancy

Planets play an important role in geomancy, the study of the earth's energy field. By observing the positions of the planets, geomancers can identify patterns and relationships that can be used to interpret the earth's energy and make predictions about future events. The planets also influence the flow of energy within the earth, and by understanding these influences, geomancers can adjust their practices to maximize the positive effects of this energy.

In addition, the planets can be used as tools for divination that provide insight into the hidden forces at work in our lives. By understanding the symbolism and meaning of each planet, we can begin to understand the messages that the earth is trying to communicate to us.

How Planets Influence Geomantic Readings

Geomantic readings are used to interpret the energy of a specific location. This practice dates back centuries and is based on the belief that the land has a unique energy signature. By understanding this signature, we can gain insights into a particular place's past, present, and future. Many different factors can influence a geomantic reading, but one of the most important is the position of the planets.

Each planet has its energy, and when they are in alignment with certain points on the earth, they can amplify or diminish the power of that location. For example, if Mars is in alignment with a powerful geomantic point, it can intensify the energy of that point. Conversely, if Saturn is in alignment with a point of weakness, it can help dissipate its power. By taking the position of the planets into account, we can get a more accurate reading of the earth's energy signature.

Why Understanding Astrological Concepts Is Important for Geomancy

Astrology is the study of the movements and relative positions of celestial bodies interpreted as having an influence on human affairs and the natural world. The word "astrology" comes from the Greek words for "star" and "logos," which means "the word of God." Astrology has been used for centuries to help people understand the world around them, and it is still used today for a variety of purposes.

One of the key concepts of geomancy is the importance of understanding astrological principles. This is because the planets and stars have a tremendous impact on the Earth's energy field. By understanding how the planets and stars influence the Earth's energy, geomancers can make more informed decisions about where to place ley lines, align sacred sites, and maximize the benefits of planetary energies.

In addition, a thorough understanding of astrology can help geomancers predict potential problems and take steps to avoid them. As such, astrology is an essential tool for anyone interested in pursuing geomancy. The connection between these two ancient practices is undeniable. By understanding both, we can develop a deeper understanding of the earth's energy and position in it.

In the following sections, we will take a look at individual planets and how their energies influence geomancy.

The Sun: The Heart of Geomancy

Effects: Life-giving, Creative, Vital, Willpower

The sun is the most important planet in geomancy. It is the source of all life, and its energy is essential when it comes to sustaining the Earth's natural balance. The sun represents ego and willpower. When the sun is strong in a reading, it indicates that the individual has the potential to achieve great things. However, if the sun is weak, it indicates that the individual may need to put in more effort to realize their goals.

The sun's energy is also associated with creativity and self-expression. When the sun is strong, it indicates that the individual has the potential to create something beautiful or to bring their unique talents to the world. However, if the sun is weak, it indicates that the individual may need to put in more effort to bring their creative vision to fruition.

The sun is also associated with vitality and health. When the sun is strong, it indicates that the individual has the potential to enjoy good health and vitality. However, if the sun is weak, it indicates that the individual may need to take better care of their health and put in more effort to maintain their vitality.

Symbolism

The sun is represented by a circle with a point in the center. This symbolizes the sun's life-giving energy and its creative potential. The sun is also associated with the color gold, which represents the sun's power and vitality. The sun is also associated with the element fire. This represents the sun's energy and its ability to transform and create.

Zodiac Signs Ruled by the Sun: Aries, Leo

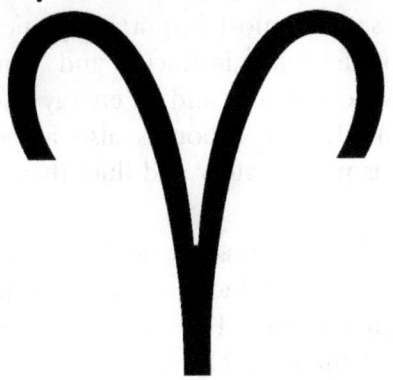

Aries is ruled by the sun.
https://pixabay.com/images/id-36388/

The Sun is considered to be the ruling planet of Leo. Leo is represented by the lion. People born under this sign are often said to be bold, ambitious, and confident. People ruled by the sun are also said to be natural leaders and are often very good at inspiring others. If you know someone who was born under the sign of Leo, you might find that they have a strong personality and are always up for a challenge.

The sun is also considered to be the ruling planet of Aries. It is represented by the ram. People born under this sign are often said to be impulsive, courageous, and competitive. People ruled by the sun are also said to be natural leaders and are often very good at taking charge. If you know someone born under Aries, you might find that they have a strong personality and are always up for a challenge.

Summary of the Sun

The sun is the most important planet in geomancy. It is the source of all life, and its energy is essential for sustaining the Earth's natural balance. The sun is a planet that should be approached with caution. Its energy is very powerful, and if it is not used correctly, it can hurt the individual's life.

In general, the sun is a positive influence on reading. Its energy is associated with growth, creativity, and self-expression. However, the sun can also be a difficult planet to handle. Its energy is very powerful, and if it is not used correctly, it can lead to egotism, narcissism, and a sense of entitlement.

Moon – Our Nearest Neighbor

Effects: Emotions, Gut Instincts, Nurturing, Feminine Energy

The moon is the second most important planet in geomancy. It is associated with emotions, gut instincts, and nurturing. The moon represents the subconscious mind, and its energy is often more powerful than the conscious mind. The moon is also associated with feminine energy, and its energy is more watery and fluid than the masculine one of the sun.

The moon's energy is more passive and receptive than that of the sun. The moon is associated with intuition and feelings, and its energy is more compassionate and nurturing. The moon's energy is also more nightmarish than that of the sun. The moon is associated with addiction, obsession, and mental illness.

Symbolism

The moon is represented by a crescent, symbolizing the moon's connection to emotions and intuition. It is also associated with the color silver. This represents the moon's connection to emotions and intuition. It is also associated with the element water. It represents the moon's fluid and changeable energy.

Zodiac Signs Ruled by the Moon: Cancer, Pisces

The moon is the ruling planet of cancer.
https://pixabay.com/images/id-2551431/

The moon is considered to be the ruling planet of Cancer, represented by the crab. People born under this sign are often emotional, intuitive, and nurturing. People ruled by the moon are also very in tune with their feelings and are often quite good at understanding other people's emotions.

The moon is also considered to be the ruling planet of Pisces. The fish represent Pisces. People born under this sign are often compassionate, adaptable, and imaginative. This sign is said to be the most intuitive of all the zodiac signs, and people ruled by the moon are often very in tune with their emotions.

Summary of the Moon

The moon is the second most important planet in geomancy. It is associated with emotions, gut instincts, and nurturing. The moon represents the subconscious mind, and its energy is often more powerful than the conscious mind. The moon is also associated with feminine energy, and its energy is more watery and fluid than the masculine one of the sun.

In general, the moon is a positive influence in readings. Its energy is associated with intuition, compassion, and creativity. However, the moon can also be a difficult planet to handle. Its energy is very powerful, and if it is not used correctly, it can lead to addiction, obsession, and mental illness.

Mercury – The Messenger

Effects: Communication, Intelligence, Travel

Mercury is the third most important planet in geomancy. It is associated with communication, intelligence, and travel. Mercury represents the conscious mind, and its energy is often more active and analytical than the subconscious mind. Mercury is also associated with the element of air. This represents Mercury's connection to communication and ideas.

Mercury's energy is more mental than emotional. This planet is associated with logic and reason, and its energy is more cerebral than the emotional one of the moon. Mercury is also associated with commerce and transportation.

Symbolism

Mercury is represented by a winged messenger. This symbolizes Mercury's connection to communication and travel. It is also associated with the color green. This represents its connection to growth, fertility, and nature.

Zodiac Signs Ruled by Mercury: Gemini, Virgo

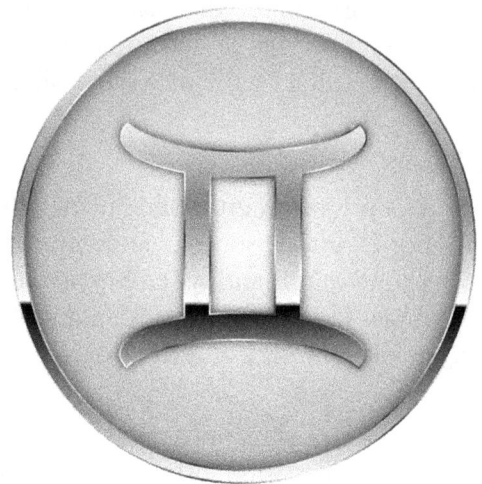

Gemini is ruled by Mercury.
https://pixabay.com/images/id-2550197/

Mercury is considered the ruling planet of Gemini and is represented by the twins. People born under this sign are often good at communication, very social, and quite adaptable. Gemini is also said to be the most intelligent of all the zodiac signs, and people ruled by Mercury are often very quick-witted and sharp.

Mercury is also considered to be the ruling planet of Virgo and is represented by the virgin. People born under this sign are often hard-working, practical, and detail-oriented. Virgo is also said to be the most grounded of all the zodiac signs, and people ruled by Mercury are often very level-headed and down-to-earth.

Summary of Mercury

Mercury is the third most important planet in geomancy. It is associated with communication, intelligence, and travel. Mercury represents the conscious mind, and its energy is often more active and analytical than the subconscious mind. Mercury is also associated with the element of air. This represents Mercury's connection to communication and ideas.

Venus – The Lover

Effects: Love, Beauty, Money

Venus is the fourth most important planet in geomancy. It is associated with love, beauty, and money. Venus represents the heart, and its energy is often more romantic and emotional than the mind. Venus is also associated with the element of earth. This represents Venus's connection to the physical world.

Symbolism

Venus is represented by the goddess of love. This symbolizes Venus's connection to love and beauty. Venus is also associated with the color pink. This represents Venus's connection to romance and femininity. With its ruling planet in the sign of Gemini, Venus brings an added element of adaptability to love and relationships.

Zodiac Signs Ruled by Venus: Taurus, Libra

Venus is the ruling planet of Taurus.
https://pixabay.com/images/id-2552502/

Venus is considered to be the ruling planet of Taurus, represented by the bull. People born under this sign are often reliable, patient, and hard-working. Taurus is also said to be the most down-to-earth of all the zodiac signs, and people ruled by Venus are often very sensual and materialistic.

Venus is also considered to be the ruling planet of Libra. Libra is represented by scales. People born under this sign are often diplomatic, fair-minded, and social. Libra is also said to be the most idealistic of all the zodiac signs, and people ruled by Venus are often very romantic and good at relationships.

Summary of Venus

Venus is associated with love, beauty, and money. Venus represents the heart, and its energy is often more romantic and emotional than the mind. Venus is also associated with the element of earth. This represents Venus' connection to the physical world. With its ruling planet in the sign of Gemini, Venus brings an added element of adaptability to love and relationships.

Mars – The Warrior

Effects: Action, Energy, Passion

The planet Mars is named after the Roman god of war. Mars is associated with action, energy, and passion. Mars represents the will, and its energy is often forceful and aggressive. Mars is also associated with the element of fire. This represents Mars' connection to energy and passion. It is also associated with the color red. This represents Mars' connection to action and assertiveness.

Symbolism

Mars is represented by the god of war. This symbolizes Mars' connection to action and aggression. Mars is also associated with iron. This represents its connection to strength and power. The symbol for Mars is a spear, which represents Mars' connection to assertiveness and courage.

Zodiac Signs Ruled by Mars: Aries, Scorpio

Mars is considered the ruling planet of Scorpio.
https://pixabay.com/images/id-2782164/

Mars is considered to be the ruling planet of Aries. It is represented by the ram. People born under this sign are often impulsive, enthusiastic, and competitive. Aries is also said to be the most independent of all the zodiac signs, and people ruled by Mars are often very self-assertive and headstrong.

Mars is also considered to be the ruling planet of Scorpio. Scorpio is represented by the scorpion. People born under this sign are often intense, passionate, and resourceful. Scorpio is also said to be the most mysterious of all the zodiac signs, and people ruled by Mars are often very private and secretive.

Summary of Mars

Mars is associated with action, energy, and passion. It represents the will, and its energy is often forceful and aggressive. Mars is also associated with the element fire. This represents Mars' connection to energy and passion. With its ruling planet in the sign of Aries, Mars brings an added element of independence to action and assertiveness.

Jupiter – The Planet of Luck

Effects: Expansion, Optimism, Opportunity

The planet Jupiter is named after the Roman god of luck. Jupiter is associated with expansion, optimism, and opportunity. It represents the principle of growth, and its energy is often optimistic and generous. Jupiter is also associated with the element of fire. This represents Jupiter's connection to growth and expansion. The color purple is also associated with Jupiter. This represents its connection to wisdom and knowledge.

Symbolism

The symbol for Jupiter is a thunderbolt, which represents Jupiter's connection to power and authority. Jupiter is also associated with tin. This represents its connection to luck and fortune. Thursday is also associated with Jupiter. This represents its connection to abundance and prosperity.

Zodiac Signs Ruled by Jupiter: Sagittarius, Pisces

Pisces is ruled by Jupiter.
https://pixabay.com/images/id-2782348/

Jupiter is considered to be the ruling planet of Sagittarius. Sagittarius is represented by the archer. People born under this sign are often optimistic, independent, and adventurous. Sagittarius is also the most idealistic of all the zodiac signs. People ruled by Jupiter are often very positive and strongly believe in justice.

Jupiter is also considered to be the ruling planet of Pisces. Pisces is represented by the fish. People born under this sign are often compassionate, imaginative, and sensitive. Pisces is also the most spiritual of all the zodiac signs, and people ruled by Jupiter are often very intuitive and in touch with their higher selves.

Summary of Jupiter

Jupiter is associated with expansion, optimism, and opportunity. Jupiter represents the principle of growth, and its energy is often optimistic and generous. Jupiter is also associated with the element of fire. This represents Jupiter's connection to growth and expansion. With its ruling planet in the sign of Sagittarius, Jupiter brings an added element of adventure and idealism to action.

Saturn – The Planet of Responsibility

Effects: Structure, Discipline, Restriction

The planet Saturn is named after the Roman god of time. Saturn is associated with structure, discipline, and restriction. Saturn represents the principle of limitation, and its energy is often serious and sober. Saturn is also associated with the element of earth. This represents Saturn's connection to stability and endurance. The color black is also associated with Saturn. This represents its connection to darkness and mystery.

Symbolism

The symbol for Saturn is a cross, which represents its connection to responsibility and duty. It is also associated with lead. This represents Saturn's connection to heaviness and density. Saturday is also associated with Saturn. This represents its connection to structure and discipline.

Zodiac Signs Ruled by Saturn: Capricorn, Aquarius

Aquarius is ruled by Saturn.
https://pixabay.com/images/id-3915988/

Saturn is considered to be the ruling planet of Capricorn. Capricorn is represented by the goat. People under this sign are often ambitious, hardworking, and practical. Capricorn is also the most disciplined of all the zodiac signs, and people ruled by Saturn are often very responsible and reliable.

Saturn is also considered to be the ruling planet of Aquarius. It is represented by the water bearer. People born under this sign are often humanitarian, progressive, and eccentric. Aquarius is also the most unconventional of all the zodiac signs, and people ruled by Saturn are often very independent and original.

Summary of Saturn

Saturn is associated with structure, discipline, and responsibility. It represents the principle of limitation, and its energy is often serious and sober. Saturn is also associated with the element earth. This represents its connection to stability and endurance. With its ruling planet in the sign of Capricorn, Saturn brings an added element of ambition and practicality to action.

Lunar Nodes – The Dragon's Head and Tail

The Lunar Nodes are two points in space where the Moon's orbit intersects with the Earth's orbit around the Sun. The point where the orbits intersect is called the node. The Lunar Nodes are also sometimes referred to as the Dragon's Head and Tail.

The North Node is considered the Dragon's Head, and the South Node is considered the Dragon's Tail. The North Node is associated with future potential, and the South Node is associated with *experience*.

The Lunar Nodes are also said to be the points of karmic destiny. The North Node is said to represent our soul's mission in this lifetime, and the South Node is said to represent our soul's karma from past lifetimes.

Symbolism

The symbol for the Lunar Nodes is two circles connected by a line. The line represents the path of destiny, and the circles represent the Dragon's Head and Tail. The North Node is associated with the element fire, and the South Node is associated with the element of water. This represents the opposing energies of the Lunar Nodes.

Zodiac Signs Ruled by the Lunar Nodes: Cancer, Capricorn

Capricon is ruled by the lunar nodes.
https://pixabay.com/images/id-2782396/

The Lunar Nodes are said to be the rulers of Cancer and Capricorn. Cancer is represented by the crab. People born under this sign are often emotional, sensitive, and nurturing. Cancer is also a sign of the home, and people ruled by the Lunar Nodes are often very family-oriented.

The goat represents Capricorn, and people born under this sign are often ambitious, hard-working, and practical. Capricorn is also a sign of responsibility, and people ruled by the Lunar Nodes are often very reliable.

Summary of the Lunar Nodes

The Lunar Nodes are not planets, but they are considered to be very important points in space. They are said to have a powerful influence on our lives and are often studied in astrology and karma. The Lunar Nodes are said to be the points of karmic destiny and represent our soul's mission in this lifetime.

The planets and other celestial bodies profoundly influence our lives, both in terms of our personalities and the larger events that shape our world. By understanding the planets' symbolism and meaning, we can better understand ourselves and the universe around us.

Chapter 3: The Elements and the Zodiac Signs

Do you ever wonder why people act the way they do? Or why you are drawn to certain types of people? Perhaps it has something to do with the stars. In this chapter, we will explore the spiritual side of zodiac signs and discover the meaning behind each element.

There are four elements in astrology, fire, earth, air, and water. Each element is associated with a set of qualities. All zodiac signs belong to one of these elements. This chapter is divided into four sections, one for each element. We will begin with a general overview of the element, followed by a keywords list, symbol, and description of the associated zodiac signs.

All zodiac signs fall under an element.
https://pixabay.com/es/photos/reloj-hist%c3%b3rico-praga-ciudad-1096054/

You will learn about the keywords, symbols, and traits associated with fire (Aries, Leo, and Sagittarius), earth (Taurus, Virgo, and Capricorn), air (Gemini, Libra, and Aquarius), and water (Cancer, Pisces, and Scorpio) zodiac signs. By the end of this chapter, you will have a greater understanding of yourself and others.

Spiritual Meaning of Zodiac Signs

Each zodiac sign has its own unique set of characteristics and traits. But did you know that each one has a spiritual meaning as well? For example, Aries is associated with new beginnings, while Pisces is associated with compassion and forgiveness.

By understanding your zodiac sign's spiritual meaning, you can better understand yourself and your place in the world. So, what is the spiritual meaning of your zodiac sign? Read on to find out.

Fire: Aries, Leo, and Sagittarius

Keywords: Action, Assertiveness, Passion, Creativity

Symbol of Fire Element: The Triangle

The element of fire is associated with qualities such as passion, courage, and determination. Fire signs are known for their high energy and enthusiasm. If you are drawn to people with these qualities, it is likely because you are a fire sign yourself.

Fire signs are also associated with the astrological houses of the self (First House), creativity (Fifth House), and spirituality (Ninth House). The planet Mars rules people with fire signs. The red planet is associated with energy, action, and assertiveness.

Zodiac Signs Associated with Fire

Three zodiac signs are associated with fire, Aries, Leo, and Sagittarius. People of these signs are said to be passionate, dynamic, and full of energy. They tend to be natural leaders and are often drawn to careers that involve taking risks. People with these signs are also known for their sense of adventure and may enjoy traveling or engaging in outdoor activities.

While people with these zodiac signs can be warm and loving, they can also be quick-tempered and impulsive. However, their fierce determination and optimistic attitude usually help them overcome any obstacle that comes their way.

Aries

Traits: Adventurous, Natural Leaders, Determined

Aries is the first sign of the zodiac, and it is associated with new beginnings. People who have this sign are said to be natural leaders. They are often drawn to careers that involve taking risks and may enjoy traveling or engaging in outdoor activities.

Aries people are also known for their sense of adventure and may be impulsive and quick-tempered. However, their fierce determination and optimistic attitude usually help them overcome any obstacle that comes their way.

Symbolism: The Ram

The symbol for Aries is a ram, which represents assertiveness, courage, and determination. In Greek mythology, the ram was associated with Olympus, the home of the gods. This connection gives Aries an added sense of nobility and grandeur. Whether you are an Aries yourself or you know someone who is, you can not help but be drawn to their energy and strength of character.

Leo

Traits: Generous, Creative, Warm-hearted, Loyal

Leo is the fifth sign of the zodiac and is associated with the astrological house of creativity (Fifth House). People who have this sign are creative and warm-hearted. They tend to be natural leaders and are often drawn to careers that involve taking risks.

People with these signs are also known for their sense of adventure and may enjoy traveling or engaging in outdoor activities. While people with these zodiac signs can be impulsive and quick-tempered, their fierce determination and optimistic attitude usually help them overcome any obstacle that comes their way.

Symbolism: The Lion

The lion is the symbol of Leo, and it represents courage, strength, and royalty. The lion is a noble creature that is often associated with the sun. In Greek mythology, the lion was also associated with Olympus, the home of the gods. The link between Leo and the sun gives Leo an added sense of warmth and generosity.

Sagittarius

Traits: Independent, Optimistic, Truth-seekers

Sagittarius is the ninth sign of the zodiac and is associated with the astrological house of spirituality (Ninth House). People who have this sign are independent and optimistic. They tend to be natural truth-seekers and are often drawn to careers that involve taking risks.

People with this sign are known for their sense of humor and their love of travel. Sagittarius is a fire sign, and the planet Jupiter rules people with this sign. Jupiter is associated with good fortune, expansion, and abundance.

Symbolism: The Archer

The archer is the symbol of Sagittarius, and it represents truth-seeking and optimism. The archer is also associated with the planet Jupiter, which gives Sagittarius its upbeat attitude. With the archer as their symbol, people with this sign always aim for the stars.

Earth: (Taurus, Virgo, and Capricorn)

Keywords: Grounded, Practical, Reliable

Symbol of the Earth: The Pentacle

Earth signs are grounded, practical, and reliable. They are often drawn to careers that involve helping others and may enjoy working with their hands. People with these signs are patient and methodical but can also be inflexible and stubborn.

Earth signs are ruled by the planet Saturn, which is associated with discipline, responsibility, and hard work. The symbol for earth is a pentacle, which represents the material world. A pentacle is a five-pointed star that is enclosed in a circle. The star's five points represent the five elements: earth, air, fire, water, and spirit.

In Greek mythology, the earth was associated with Demeter, the goddess of the harvest. Demeter was a kind and generous goddess, but she could also be stern and inflexible. The link between the earth and Demeter gives those with earth signs their practical and reliable nature.

Taurus

Traits: Reliable, Patient, Practical, Sensual

Taurus is the second sign of the zodiac and is associated with the astrological house of material possessions (Second House). People who have this sign are reliable and patient. They tend to be practical and down-to-earth and are often drawn to careers that involve security and stability.

People with this sign are also known for their love of sensual pleasures. Taurus is an earth sign, and people with this sign are ruled by the planet Venus. Venus is associated with love, beauty, and pleasure. It is also linked to the goddess Aphrodite, who was known for her beauty and sensuality.

Symbolism: The Bull

The bull is the symbol of Taurus, and it represents dependability, patience, and practicality. The bull is also associated with the planet Venus, which gives Taurus its love of beauty and pleasure. The bull is a gentle creature but can also be stubborn and inflexible. This combination of qualities makes Taurus a reliable and down-to-earth sign.

Virgo

Traits: Analytical, Loyal, Hardworking, Practical

Virgo is the sixth sign of the zodiac and is associated with the astrological house of work and health (Sixth House). People who have this sign are analytical and hard-working. They tend to be loyal and practical and are often drawn to careers that involve helping others.

People with this sign are also known for their attention to detail. Virgo is an earth sign, and people with this sign are ruled by the planet Mercury. Mercury is associated with communication, commerce, and travel. It is also linked to the god Hermes, who was known for his cunning and wit.

Symbolism: The Virgin

The virgin is the symbol of Virgo, and it represents purity, innocence, and virginity. The virgin is also associated with the planet Mercury, which gives Virgo its attention to detail and analytical mind. The virgin is a pure and innocent creature, but can also be complex and mysterious. This combination of qualities makes Virgo an analytical and hard-working sign.

Capricorn

Traits: Ambitious, Driven, Persistent, Resourceful

Capricorn is the tenth sign of the zodiac and is associated with the astrological house of career and ambition (Tenth House). People who have this sign are ambitious and driven. They tend to be persistent and resourceful and are often drawn to careers involving power and status.

People with this sign are also known for their discipline and self-control. Capricorn is an earth sign, and people with this sign are ruled by the planet Saturn. Saturn is associated with responsibility, hard work, and discipline. It is also linked to the god Cronus, who was known for his strength and power.

Symbolism: The Goat

The goat is the symbol of Capricorn, and it represents ambition, persistence, and resourcefulness. The goat is also associated with the planet Saturn, which gives Capricorn its discipline and self-control. The goat is a hard-working and determined creature, but it can also be stubborn and inflexible. This combination of qualities makes Capricorn an ambitious and driven sign.

Air: Gemini, Libra, Aquarius

Keywords: Communication, Intellectualism, Social Interactions.

Symbol for the Air Element: The Winged Messenger

Air signs are associated with the astrological houses of communication (Third House) and social interactions (Eleventh House). People with air signs are often known for their communication skills and intellectualism. They tend to be social and outgoing and are often drawn to careers involving networking and social interactions.

The symbol for air is the winged messenger, who represents communication and intellectualism. The messenger is also associated with the planet Mercury, which gives air signs the communication skills and social nature. The messenger is a quick and agile creature, but it can also be scattered and unfocused in nature. It is this combination of qualities that makes air signs social and intellectual.

Gemini

Traits: Adaptable, Communicative, Inquisitive, Social

Gemini is the third sign of the zodiac and is associated with the astrological house of communication (Third House). People with this sign are known for their communication skills and inquisitive nature. They tend to be adaptable and social and are often drawn to careers involving networking and social interactions.

People with this sign are also known for their dual nature. Gemini is an air sign, and people with this sign are ruled by the planet Mercury. Mercury is associated with communication, commerce, and travel. It is also linked to the god Hermes, who was known for his cunning and wit.

Symbolism: The Twins

The twins are the symbol of Gemini and represent communication and duality. The twins are also associated with the planet Mercury, which gives Gemini its communication skills and inquisitive nature. The twins are quick and agile creatures but can also be scattered and unfocused. This combination of qualities makes Gemini an adaptable and communicative sign.

Libra

Traits: Balanced, Diplomatic, Fair-minded, Social

Libra is the seventh sign of the zodiac and is associated with the astrological house of relationships (Seventh House). People with this sign are often known for their diplomacy and social nature. They tend to be fair-minded and balanced and are often drawn to careers involving networking and social interactions.

People with this sign are also known for their indecision. Libra is an air sign, and people with this sign are ruled by the planet Venus. Venus is associated with love, beauty, and relationships. It is also linked to the goddess Aphrodite, who was known for her beauty and charm.

Symbolism: The Scales

The scales are Libra's symbol, representing balance and relationships. The scales are also associated with the planet Venus, which gives Libra its diplomatic and social nature. The scales are a stable and reliable creature, but they can also be indecisive and changeable. This combination of qualities makes Libra a balanced and fair-minded sign.

Aquarius

Traits: Eccentric, Friendly, Humanitarian, Independent

Aquarius is the eleventh sign of the zodiac, and it is associated with the astrological house of social interactions (Eleventh House). People with this sign are often known for their eccentricity and humanitarianism. They tend to be independent and friendly and are often drawn to careers involving networking and social interactions.

People with this sign are also known for their unpredictable nature. Aquarius is an air sign, and people with this sign are ruled by the planet Uranus. Uranus is associated with change, freedom, and innovation. It is also linked to the god Zeus, who was known for his power and strength.

Symbolism: The Water Bearer

The water bearer is the symbol of Aquarius, and it represents eccentricity and humanitarianism. The water bearer is also associated with the planet Uranus, which gives Aquarius its unpredictable nature. The water bearer is a creative and unconventional creature, but they can also be aloof and detached. This combination of qualities makes Aquarius an eccentric and independent sign.

Water: Cancer, Pisces, Scorpio

Keywords for Water Element: Emotional, Intuitive, Compassionate, Nurturing, Imaginative, Sensitive.

Symbol for the Water Element: The Cup

Water signs are associated with the astrological houses of emotions (Fourth House) and imagination (Twelfth House). People with water signs are often known for their emotions and imagination. They tend to be compassionate and nurturing and are often drawn to careers that involve caring for others.

People with water signs are also known for their sensitivity. Water signs are ruled by the planet Neptune and the Moon. The Moon is associated with emotions, while Neptune is associated with imagination. Water signs are obviously linked to the element of water, which is associated with emotions and intuition.

The cup is the symbol of water, and it represents emotions and imagination. The cup is also associated with the planet Neptune, which gives water signs their sensitivity. The cup is a receptacle for emotions, and it is also a source of nourishment. It is this combination of qualities that makes water signs compassionate and nurturing.

Cancer

Traits: Emotional, Intuitive, Compassionate, Nurturing

Cancer is the fourth sign of the zodiac and is associated with the astrological house of emotions (Fourth House). People with this sign are often known for their emotions and compassion. They tend to be nurturing and intuitive and are often drawn to careers that involve caring for others.

People with this sign are also known for their sensitivity. Cancer is a water sign, and people with this sign are ruled by the planet Moon. The Moon is associated with emotions. Cancer is also linked to the element of water, which is associated with intuition.

Symbolism: The Crab

The crab is the symbol of Cancer, and it represents emotions and compassion. The crab is also associated with the planet Moon, which gives Cancer its sensitivity. The crab is a hard-working and loyal creature but can also be moody and withdrawn. This combination of qualities makes Cancer an emotional and compassionate sign.

Pisces

Traits: Emotional, Intuitive, Compassionate, Nurturing, Imaginative

Pisces is the twelfth sign of the zodiac, and it is associated with the astrological house of imagination (Twelfth House). People with this sign are often known for their imagination and compassion. They tend to be nurturing and intuitive and are often drawn to careers that involve caring for others.

People with this sign are also known for their sensitivity. Pisces is a water sign, and the planet Neptune rules people with this sign. Neptune is associated with imagination. Pisces is also linked to the element of water, which is associated with intuition.

Symbolism: The Fish

The fish is the symbol of Pisces, and it represents imagination and compassion. The fish is also associated with the planet Neptune, which gives Pisces its sensitivity. The fish is a creative and imaginative creature but can also easily be distracted. This combination of qualities makes Pisces a compassionate and imaginative sign.

Scorpio

Traits: Emotional, Intuitive, Passionate, Nurturing, Sensitive

Scorpio is the eighth sign of the zodiac and is associated with the astrological house of emotions (Fourth House). People with this sign are often known for their emotions and passion. They tend to be nurturing and intuitive and are often drawn to careers that involve caring for others.

People with this sign are also known for their sensitivity. Scorpio is a water sign, and planet Pluto rules people with this sign. Pluto is associated with passion. Scorpio is also linked to the element of water, which is associated with intuition.

Symbolism: The Scorpion

The scorpion is Scorpio's symbol, representing passion and emotion. The scorpion is also associated with the planet Pluto, which gives Scorpio its sensitivity. The scorpion is a passionate and intense creature but can also be jealous and possessive in nature. This combination of qualities makes Scorpio a sign of passion and emotion.

The spiritual meaning of the zodiac signs and their elements can be used to help understand people's personalities. The four elements, fire, earth, air, and water represent different qualities associated with the twelve zodiac signs.

Fire signs are associated with qualities such as passion and energy, while earth signs are associated with qualities such as stability and practicality. Air signs are associated with qualities such as intelligence and communication, while water signs are associated with qualities such as emotion and intuition.

Each sign is ruled by a planet, with each planet giving the signs their unique qualities. For example, Mars gives Aries its fiery energy, while Venus gives Libra its diplomatic charm. Neptune gives Pisces its imaginative nature, while Pluto gives Scorpio its intense passion.

By understanding the meaning of the zodiac signs and their elements, we can better understand people's personalities. People are complex, and no one sign can describe a person perfectly. However, by looking at the elements and planets associated with each sign, we can get a general idea of what qualities each one represents.

Chapter 4: The Geomantic Houses

Do you want to learn about the geomantic houses? Are you familiar with any of the 12 geomantic houses? These 12 houses originated in Babylonian astrology and were later adopted by the Greeks. They are a fundamental piece of knowledge one should have to interpret a geomantic chart. While the astrological houses deal with planetary energies, the geomantic houses deal with the energies of the Earth.

In this chapter, we will discuss the meaning and significance of the astrological houses. You will learn about the 12 houses and their rulers. We will also touch on the three "extra" geomantic houses: the two witnesses and the judge. By the end of this chapter, you will have a better understanding of the geomantic houses and how they can be used to interpret a geomantic chart.

Introduction to Geomantic Houses

If you are just getting started with geomancy, you may be wondering what all the fuss is about with these houses. After all, are they not just a way to divide the sky into manageable sections? While that is certainly one way to think about them, there is a lot more to geomantic houses than meets the eye. Understanding how to use houses is essential to interpreting a geomantic chart properly.

Each of the 12 houses corresponds to a different area of life, and each one is associated with a different planet and zodiac sign. This means that when you are looking at a geomantic chart, you can get a sense of which areas of life are being affected by which planets. For example, if you see a planet in the first house, it indicates that there are currently some major changes taking place in your life. If you see a planet in the seventh house, it indicates that relationships are playing an important role in your current situation.

Of course, this is just a very basic introduction to geomantic houses. There is a lot more to learn if you want to get the most out of this ancient system of divination. But even if you only have a basic understanding of houses, you can still use them to get valuable insights into your life.

The 12 Geomantic Houses

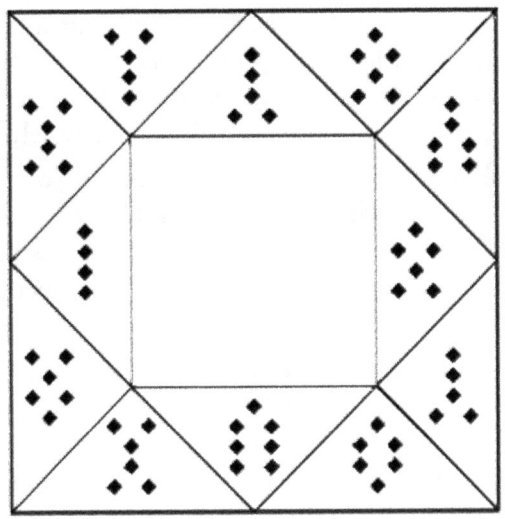

Geomantic house chart.
https://commons.wikimedia.org/wiki/File:Geomantic_housechart.svg

Now that we have briefly introduced the concept of geomantic houses, let's take a more in-depth look at each of the 12 houses. Remember, each house corresponds to a different area of life, so you will want to pay attention to the areas of your life that are most affected by the planets in each house.

The houses are each divided into three groups of four houses. The first group, known as the angular houses, comprises the 1st, 4th, 7th, and 10th houses. These are the most important houses in a geomantic chart, as they represent the areas of life that are most affected by the planets.

The second group, known as the succedent houses, comprises the 2nd, 5th, 8th, and 11th houses. These houses represent the areas of life that are the second most affected by the planets. The third group, known as the cadent houses, comprises the 3rd, 6th, 9th, and 12th houses. These houses represent the areas of life that are the least affected by the planets.

The angular houses govern the areas of life most important to you, while the cadent houses govern the areas of life least important to you. The succedent houses fall somewhere in between, governing the areas of life that are somewhat important to you. Now that you know how the houses are divided, let us look at each one in more detail.

The 1st House: House of Self

If you are looking to understand yourself better, the 1st house is a great place to start. Also known as the House of Self, this astrological house is all about your identity and how you present yourself to the world. It is also closely linked with your physical appearance, so if you want to make changes to your look, the 1st house can offer some insight into that area.

To further explore the 1st house, take a look at your birth chart. The sign occupying this house will give you clues about the areas of your life that are most important to you. For example, if Aries is in your 1st house, you may be especially driven and ambitious. Or, if Cancer is in this house, you may place a high value on family and home life.

The first house, also known as the ascendant, is associated with the planet Mars and the zodiac sign Aries. This house represents your individuality and how you relate to the world around you. By understanding the energy of the 1st house, you can better understand who you are and what makes you unique.

The 2nd House: House of Possessions

The 2nd house is all about possessions and material wealth. This includes not only your physical possessions but also your financial resources, skills and talents, and anything else you see as valuable. In a way, the 2nd house is a measure of your self-worth. Do you see yourself as wealthy or poor? Do you have a lot to offer the world, or do you feel like you have nothing to offer?

The 2nd house is also about how you handle your possessions. Are you a hoarder or a minimalist? Do you take care of your belongings, or do you let them fall into disrepair? The 2nd house reminds us that our possessions are not permanent but subject to change and misfortune. Therefore, it is important to use our possessions wisely and to remember that they are not what ultimately gives our lives value.

The 3rd House: House of Communications

The 3rd house is all about communication and the exchange of ideas. This includes spoken language, written language, body language, and any other form of communication. It also includes our relationship with knowledge and learning. Do we like to learn new things or prefer to stick to what we already know?

The 3rd house is also about our immediate environment and the people we interact with on a daily basis. This includes our siblings, our neighbors, and our co-workers. The 3rd house is a reminder that we are constantly interacting with the world around us and that our interactions significantly impact our lives.

The 4th House: House of Home and Family

The 4th house is commonly referred to as the house of home and family. This is because this house governs our domestic life, our roots, and our sense of belonging. The fourth house cusp (the line that divides the 4th house and the 3rd house) represents our childhood, and the plants in this house represent our parents and grandparents. The fourth house is also traditionally associated with the element of water, which symbolizes emotion, intuition, and creativity.

When we balance the energies of the 4th house, we create a supportive foundation for ourselves and our loved ones. We feel a sense of stability and security and express ourselves more freely. Our connection to our roots strengthens, and we nurture our relationships with others more effectively. The 4th house is a reminder that our family and home are our refuges from the outside world and that they should be treated with care.

The 5th House: House of Creativity

The fifth house is the House of Creativity, which pertains to all self-expression forms. This includes art, music, writing, and other activities that allow us to share our talents with the world. The fifth house symbolizes children and is associated with pregnancy and childbirth. In a more general sense, the fifth house represents all forms of pleasure and enjoyment. It is linked to joyful experiences such as vacations, parties, and any other form of entertainment.

When planets are located in the fifth house, they bring forth creative energies that can be used in constructive ways. However, if the planets are in challenging positions, they can create difficulties with self-expression or cause problems with fertility. Overall, the fifth house is a place of fun and creativity, and it reminds us to enjoy the good things in life.

The 6th House: House of Health and Work

The 6th house is associated with health and work. It is believed that Mercury governs this house and that Virgo is especially relevant. People with a strong 6th house influence are often hard workers who take pride in their achievements. They may be well-organized and detail-oriented, but they can also be overly perfectionist or critical.

Health is also important for people with a strong 6th house influence. They may be interested in nutrition and fitness and be careful about maintaining a healthy lifestyle. However, they can also be prone to worry and stress, which can take a toll on their physical well-being. Ultimately, the 6th house is a complex and intriguing energy field that sheds light on many aspects of our lives.

The 7th House: House of Balance

In astrology, the 7th house is associated with balance. This is the house of relationships, and it is through our relationships that we learn to find balance in our lives. The energy of the 7th house helps us see both sides of every situation and to find a middle ground between our own needs and those of others. It is also the house of compromise, teaching us that sometimes we have to give up something to gain something else.

In short, the 7th house helps us create harmony in our lives. When this house is strong in our birth chart, we can build satisfying and supportive relationships. We are also good at finding win-win solutions to conflicts.

If this house is weak in our chart, we may have difficulty seeing both sides of an issue, or we may find it hard to let go of our own needs to meet the needs of others. We may also struggle with making compromises. However, by working with the energy of the 7th house, we can learn to find balance in our lives.

The 8th House: House of Transformation

The 8th house is known as the House of Transformation. This is the house of death and rebirth, and it is associated with the planet Pluto. An 8th house is a place of power, and it is through this house that we learn to transform our lives. This house teaches us that change is an essential part of life and that we must learn to let go of the past to move forward.

The 8th house is also linked to sex, and through this house, we can learn to create new life. This house is about passion and intimacy, and it reminds us that sex is a sacred act of creation. Ultimately, the 8th house is a place of great power, and it teaches us that change is an essential part of life. If we can learn to embrace the energy of this house, we can transform our lives in profound and wonderful ways.

The 9th House: House of Higher Learning

The 9th house is associated with higher learning, and those who have planets in this house are often drawn to fields of study that require deep understanding and concentration. This may include academic subjects such as philosophy, religion, or the law. But it also encompasses more creative pursuits such as literature, poetry, and art.

Those with planets in the 9th house often have a deep need to explore the big questions in life, and they may find themselves spending hours lost in thought or absorbed in contemplation. To the outside world, they may appear aloof or even arrogant, but this is simply their way of processing the information they take in. They are constantly seeking knowledge, and their minds are always whirring with new ideas.

The 10th House: House of Career

The 10th House is commonly referred to as the House of Career. This is because it is associated with professional achievements, reputation, and public status. In a birth chart, the 10th House is located on the Midheaven, which is the highest point in the sky. This position symbolizes our highest aspirations and ambitions.

The planets and signs that occupy the 10th House reveal how we will go about achieving our goals and what kind of success we are likely to experience. For example, a planet in the 10th House may indicate that we will achieve our goals through our hard work and perseverance. Alternatively, a planet in this House may suggest that we will receive help from influential people or that we will have a natural talent for a particular profession.

Regardless of the planets involved, the 10th House always represents our drive to achieve success in the public eye. Through this House, we learn to take our place in the world and make our mark on society.

The 11th House: House of Friendships

In astrology, the 11th House is known as the House of Friendships. It represents our social circle and the relationships we have with others. This House is all about connection and community. We often think of our friends as family, and this house reflects just that. It reminds us that we are part of a larger community and that we need to nurture our friendships.

The 11th House also represents our hopes and dreams. This is the House of our wishes and aspirations. We all have a vision for our future, and the 11th House reminds us to pursue those dreams. When we align our actions with our intentions, we can make powerful changes in our lives. So, the next time you feel lonely, remember that you have a whole community of friends waiting for you in the 11th House.

The 12th House: House of the Unconscious

The 12th house is often referred to as the "house of the unconscious." This is because it represents the parts of ourselves that we are not usually aware of. This includes our hidden fears, desires, and motivations. The 12th house also represents our karma and past lives. This is why it is sometimes called the "house of self-undoing."

The positive side of the 12th house is that it can help us understand ourselves on a deeper level. By exploring our shadow selves, we can learn to accept and forgive ourselves. We can also gain insights into our past lives and how they are influencing our present situation. However, the 12th house can also be a difficult place to confront our demons. It is important to approach this house with caution and insight, or we may find ourselves lost in its depths.

Extra Geomantic Houses

In addition to the 12 astrological houses, there are also three geomantic houses. These are the houses of the two witnesses and the judge. These houses are used to further understand the chart as a whole. The two witnesses represent the opposing forces at work in the chart, while the judge represents the outcome.

The Two Witnesses

The two witnesses are traditionally represented by the Sun and Moon. They represent the two opposing forces at work in the chart. The Sun represents our conscious mind, while the Moon represents our unconscious mind. These two forces are always in conflict with each other. The Sun wants us to take action and pursue our goals, while the Moon wants us to stay safe and comfortable. This conflict is what makes us human.

The 1st Witness: House of Beginning

The 1st Witness is associated with the beginning of anything, which makes it an important part of any geomantic reading. This house represents all that is new, fresh, and exciting. It is a time of potential and possibility when anything seems possible. The 1st Witness encourages us to take risks and to venture into the unknown. It is a time of exploration and adventure when we are open to new experiences.

This house reminds us that every journey begins with a single step and that even the smallest act can have significance. So, whatever you are embarking on, remember that the 1st Witness is with you, urging you to take that first step into the great unknown.

The 2nd Witness: House of Progress

The 2nd Witness is associated with progress and forward momentum. This house represents our ability to move forward in life and to make progress towards our goals. It is a time of growth and expansion when we are expanding our horizons. The 2nd Witness reminds us that even when things are tough, we can always find a way to move forward. This house is a reminder that we are never stuck in one place and that there is always room for growth.

This house is a reminder that even when we feel lost, we can always find our way again. So, if you are feeling lost, remember that the 2nd Witness is with you, urging you to keep moving forward.

The Judge: House of Conclusion

The Judge is associated with conclusion and resolution. This house represents our ability to bring things to a close. It is a time of endings and closure when we can let go of the past. The Judge reminds us that even though things may end, there is always something new waiting for us around the corner. This house serves as a reminder that even when things seem dark, there is always a light at the end of the tunnel. So, if you are feeling down, remember that the Judge is with you, urging you to keep going.

The geomantic houses are a fundamental part of any geomantic reading. They provide insight into the various forces at work in the chart and how they interact with each other. By understanding these houses, we can gain a better understanding of our own lives and the world around us.

The houses are divided into 12 astrological houses and three extra geomantic houses. The houses are classified into three groups, the angular houses, the succedent houses, and the cadent houses. The angular houses are the 1st, 4th, 7th, and 10th houses. The succedent houses are the 2nd, 5th, 8th, and 11th houses. The cadent houses are the 3rd, 6th, 9th, and 12th houses.

The astrological houses represent the various areas of our lives, while the extra geomantic houses represent the opposing forces at work in the chart and the outcome. The houses are a reminder that we are constantly moving forward and that there is always room for growth. So, whatever you are going through, remember that the houses are with you, urging you to keep moving forward.

Chapter 5: Preparing Your Mind

To interpret the messages that come to you through geomancy, it is crucial to have a clear mind. The symbols that appear in a geomantic reading can be open to interpretation, and it is important to be able to see them clearly to find the meaning that is most relevant to you.

It's important to have a clear mind with geomancy.
https://pixabay.com/es/photos/hombre-ma%c3%b1ana-amanecer-sentado-2264051/

If your mind is cluttered with worries or distractions, it will be difficult to find the clarity you need. To get the most out of a geomantic reading, take some time beforehand to clear your mind and focus on what you hope to learn. By taking this step, you will be setting yourself up for success.

This chapter will give you some ideas and tips for how to prepare beforehand so that you can get the most out of your geomancy readings.

Preparing for Geomancy

There are many different ways to prepare for a geomancy session, but the most important thing is to make sure that you are comfortable and relaxed. You may want to sit or lie down in a quiet place where you will not be disturbed. You may also want to spend a few minutes meditating or doing some other form of relaxation exercise to clear your mind.

Once you are ready, you can begin to focus on your breath and the energy of the earth. Allow yourself to sink into the ground and become one with the earth's energy. Once you feel connected, you can start to explore the different ways you can use this energy to improve your life.

Here are some steps you can take to prepare for a geomancy session:

1. Clearing Your Mind

The first step is to clear your mind. Over time, our subconscious mind accumulates a lot of mental clutter, and it can be helpful to take some time to declutter before starting a geomancy session. You can do this by focusing on your breath and observing every thought that comes into your mind without judgment. Once you have become more aware of your thoughts, you can start to let go of the ones that are no longer serving you.

Carrying the baggage from your past will only weigh you down and make it difficult to move forward. Take some time to release any thoughts or emotions you have not dealt with yet. If you need help, there are many resources available that can guide you through the process of clearing your mind. Do not leave this step until the last minute. It can take some time to achieve a state of mental clarity.

2. Connecting with the Earth

It is important to first establish a connection with the Earth to prepare for a geomantic reading. This can be done in many ways, but one simple method is to sit or stand barefoot outside on the ground for a few minutes. As you focus on your breath, feel the Earth's grounding energy entering your body through your feet. Place your hands directly on the ground or hold a piece of raw crystal in each hand.

There are many different ways to work with natural elements to prepare for a geomancy reading. One simple method is to spend time outside in nature, paying attention to the patterns around you. Notice how the leaves blow in the wind, the branches grow on trees, and the water flows in a river. These patterns can offer guidance and insight into your life.

Once you feel connected to the Earth, you can begin to still your mind and open yourself up to receive guidance from the natural world around you. Trust that the answers you seek will be revealed to you through the patterns of the rocks, trees, and other elements in the landscape. You may also want to ask the Earth for help in understanding the messages you receive.

3. Developing Your Intuition

Geomancers work with the land to connect with its spirit and bring about positive change. To become a geomancer, it is essential to develop your intuition. Intuition is a form of knowing the things that go beyond the five senses. It is a way of accessing knowledge that is not available through logical reasoning.

There are many different ways to develop your intuition. One simple method is to spend time each day practicing meditation or mindfulness. As you focus on your breath and still your mind, you will begin to notice the subtle thoughts and feelings that arise. With practice, you will be able to quiet your mind and focus more easily on your intuition.

To develop your intuition, begin by spending time in nature. Connect with the earth beneath your feet and heed the guidance that comes into your heart. You may also find it useful to work with a mentor who can help you hone your skills. With practice, you will develop the ability to read the earth's energy and use it to bring about positive change.

You can also develop your intuition by paying attention to your dreams. Keep a dream journal and write down the details of your dreams as soon as you wake up. Over time, you will begin to notice patterns and symbols that mean something to you. These messages can offer guidance and insight into your life.

4. Protecting Yourself Spiritually

Anyone interested in pursuing geomantic readings should take some time to prepare themselves spiritually. This means creating a safe space where you can focus on your reading without any outside distractions. It also means being aware of your energy and how it might affect the reading.

One simple way to protect yourself spiritually is to create an altar. An altar can be as simple or as elaborate as you like. It can be a dedicated space in your home or a portable box you take with you when traveling. Fill your altar with items that represent your intention for the reading. You might include crystals, herbs, photos, or symbols that have meaning for you.

Another way to protect yourself spiritually is to cleanse your energy before you begin. This can be done with a salt bath, by smudging with sage, or by using any other method you feel drawn to. The important thing is to cleanse your space and yourself so that you can approach the reading with a clear mind.

You may also want to meditate or do some other type of relaxation exercise to clear your mind and open yourself up to the experience. And finally, it is important to set an intention for the reading. What do you hope to learn? What are you looking for guidance on? By taking some time to prepare mentally and emotionally, you will be able to get the most out of your geomantic reading.

5. Doing Daily Exercises

You can do a few exercises every day to help you on your journey to becoming a geomancer. By taking time each day to focus on your breath and connect with your body, you will start to develop a deeper understanding of your energy field. This will be helpful when it comes time to read the energy of a space or person.

Daily exercises will help ground and center you, making it easier to receive clear information during readings. They will also protect you from outside influences that can disrupt your reading. Make sure to set aside some time each day to focus on your practice. If you are unsure where to start, plenty of resources are available online or in your local library.

6. Noticing Recurring Patterns

As you work with geomancy, you will start noticing patterns in the world around you. It is vital to become attuned to recurring patterns in both the physical and abstract worlds. By doing this, you will be able to easily find the symbols that will give you information about the issue at hand.

To begin, take some time each day to notice the patterns around you, both in your immediate environment and in the larger world. Pay attention to how the light falls on objects, how shadows are cast, and how people and animals move through space. As you become more attuned to these patterns, you will start to see them everywhere, providing you with a wealth of information to work with during your readings.

Meditation Exercises

Meditation plays an important role in the practice of geomancy. Through meditation, you will develop a deeper understanding of your energy and how it interacts with the world around you. There are many different ways to meditate, so find a method that works for you and stick with it. Here are a few basic exercises to get you started.

1. Grounding Meditation

This meditation is designed to help you connect with the earth and ground your energy. It is a simple exercise that can be done anywhere, at any time. We must first ground ourselves in meditation to read the earth's energy. This will help us to clear our minds and open our hearts to the earth's wisdom.

To begin, find a comfortable place to sit or lie down. Close your eyes and take a few deep breaths. Imagine roots growing from your feet, connecting you to the earth's center. Feel the earth's energy entering your body, filling you with strength and grounding you in your power. Allow yourself to be still, at peace, and receptive to the earth's guidance. When you are ready, open your eyes and begin your reading.

2. Intuition Meditation

This meditation is designed to help you connect with your intuition and the unseen world. It will allow you to access the knowledge and guidance available to you. The exercise is simple, but it may take some time to master. Be patient with yourself and trust that you will receive the information you need.

To begin, find a comfortable place to sit or lie down in. Close your eyes and take a few deep breaths. Imagine yourself surrounded by a bright, white light. This light is filled with wisdom and knowledge and is here to guide you. Allow yourself to relax and receive the light's guidance. When you are ready, open your eyes and begin your reading.

3. Visualization

One of the most important steps in preparing for geomantic readings is to learn how to visualize. This skill is essential for reading the patterns formed by the lines and shapes in the sand. The ability to clearly see these patterns will allow you to interpret them more easily and make more accurate readings. With practice, it will become second nature, and you will be able to do it without even thinking.

To develop your visualization skills, find a quiet place where you can comfortably sit or lie down. Close your eyes and take a few deep breaths. Begin to picture the lines and shapes in your mind's eye. As you become more comfortable with visualization, you will be able to see the patterns clearly. With practice, you will be able to interpret the meaning of these patterns and use them to make predictions.

4. Mantras

Mantras are sacred syllables or phrases used as a tool for meditation. When recited correctly, mantras can help focus the mind and promote feelings of peace and well-being. For those new to mantra meditation, finding one that really resonates with you can be helpful. Once you have chosen a mantra, it is important to recite it correctly.

The correct pronunciation of mantras is said to be essential for unlocking their power. Many mantras are recorded so they can be easily and accurately learned. In addition to correct pronunciation, it is also important to recite mantras with intention. Repeat your mantra slowly and mindfully, letting the sound wash over you and fill you with positive energy. With regular practice, you will develop a deeper understanding of mantras' role in geomantic readings.

5. Mudras

Mudras are an important part of geomantic readings. They are gestures used to channel energy and focus the mind. There are many different mudras, and each has its meaning and purpose. Learning about the different mudras and how to use them is important to prepare for a geomantic reading.

The first step is to find a comfortable position. Sit with your spine straight and your legs crossed. Place your hands on your knees, palm up. Take a few deep breaths and close your eyes. Once you are settled, begin by holding the mudra for focus. Place your thumb and index finger together and extend the other fingers. Hold this mudra in front of your third eye, just above the bridge of your nose. Focus on your breath and allow your mind to become still.

Once you have achieved inner peace, you can begin the reading. Remember to keep your mind focused and open to receiving guidance from the universe. Mudras will help you to connect with the energy around you and receive accurate insights.

6. Affirmations

To get the most accurate and helpful readings, it is crucial to be mentally and emotionally prepared. One way to do this is through the use of affirmations. An affirmation is a positive statement that you repeat to yourself to program your mind for success. For example, you might say to yourself, "I am open to all the insight and guidance that the Universe has to offer."

By affirming your intention to receive guidance, you are opening yourself up to the possibility of having a successful reading. Another affirmation that you can use is "I am willing to release all fears and doubts that are holding me back." This affirmation will clear your mind and allow you to receive more fully the messages you are meant to receive.

Repeating these affirmations (or ones like them) before your reading will help to ensure that you are in the right mindset to receive accurate and helpful guidance. The better prepared you are, the more helpful your reading will be.

7. Crystals and Stones

If you are interested in having a geomantic reading done, there are a few things you can do to prepare. One of the most important things is to choose the right crystals and stones. Each type of crystal has its unique properties and energies, so it is important to choose ones that will be supportive of your specific situation.

For example, if you are looking for guidance on your career path, you might choose crystals like citrine or carnelian. If you are hoping to improve your health, you might choose crystals like amethyst or jade. And if you are seeking protection from negative energy, you might choose crystals like black tourmaline or obsidian.

By taking the time to choose the right crystals, you can ensure that your reading is both accurate and helpful. The use of crystals and stones is a powerful way to connect with the energies of the earth and receive guidance from the universe.

8. Candles

Another way to prepare for a geomantic reading is to use candles. Candles are often used in readings because they can create a peaceful and relaxing environment. They can also focus your mind and connect you with the energies of the universe.

When choosing candles for your reading, choosing ones made from natural materials like beeswax or soy is important. You should also choose candles that are scented with essential oils, as these can improve your mood and focus. If you are not sure which candles to choose, you can ask your geomancer for guidance.

The use of candles is a simple but effective way to prepare for a geomantic reading. By choosing the right candles, you can help ensure that your reading is accurate and helpful.

9. Smudging

Smudging is another way to prepare for a geomantic reading. Smudging is the practice of burning herbs and using the smoke to cleanse and purify your space. This is usually done with a bundle of dried sage, but other herbs can also be used. You can also use an essential oil diffuser or burn candles scented with cleansing oils like eucalyptus or lemon.

Many people find that smudging helps to create a more peaceful and relaxing environment. It is a powerful way to cleanse your space and prepare for a reading. It helps to clear away any negative energy that might be present, and it also helps to focus your mind and connect you with the energies of the universe.

Smudging is a simple but effective way to prepare for a geomantic reading. Taking the time to smudge your area can guarantee that your reading is correct.

10. Protection Ritual

Before your reading, it is also essential to do a protection ritual. This will protect you from any negative energy that might be present. It is crucial to create a space that is sacred and safe. There are many different ways to do this, but one simple method is to cleanse the space with sage smoke. You can also use crystals or other objects to create a circle of protection.

Once your space is ready, you can begin the reading. It is important to relax and clear your mind so that you can receive messages from the universe. Trust your intuition and allow the symbols to guide you. With preparation and an open mind, you will be able to receive the guidance you need from the natural world.

Preparing your mind for a geomantic reading is essential for receiving accurate and helpful guidance. Clearing your mind and opening yourself up to the messages of the universe will ensure that your reading is correct.

There are many different ways to prepare for a reading, but some simple methods include going out in nature, meditating, doing daily exercises, noticing recurring patterns, protecting yourself spiritually, and using candles, crystals, and smudging.

This chapter has given you a few ideas and tips for how to prepare beforehand. The meditation exercises and protection rituals at the end of this chapter will also help you get started. Remember, the most important thing is to relax and trust your intuition. With preparation and an open mind, you will be able to receive the guidance you need from the natural world.

Chapter 6: Casting the Points

Doing a geomantic reading is a lot like reading tea leaves. Geomancy uses markings in the dirt, lines, points, and dots to create figures that are then interpreted. The first step when doing a geomantic reading is casting the points. A variety of methods can be used to do this, from writing the lines randomly to throwing dice, flipping coins, or using geomancy cards.

As the lines, points, and dots are randomly placed, you can use any method. While there are many ways to cast the points, it is vital to personalize the process according to your own beliefs. This chapter will explore the various methods for casting the points and some dos and don'ts to keep in mind while doing so.

The First Step: Casting the Points

The process of casting the points is meant to create random figures that can then be interpreted for their meaning. In some cases, the points may be read directly, while in other cases, they may be used to create more complex geomantic figures. Although the interpretation of geomantic figures can be complex, the process of casting the points is relatively simple and can be done by anyone with just a bit of practice.

When casting the points, the first step is to choose a method. Various methods can be used, from writing the lines randomly to throwing dice, flipping coins, or using geomancy cards. Once a method has been chosen, the points can be cast by following the instructions for that particular method.

Whether you are looking for guidance on a personal issue or advice on a major life decision, no question is too big or small for geomancy. The only limit is your imagination.

Various Methods for Casting the Points

There are a variety of methods that can be used to cast the points. Some methods are more complex than others, but all can be used to create random figures that can then be interpreted.

1. Writing the Lines Randomly

One of the simplest methods for casting the points is to randomly draw lines randomly. This method involves drawing a series of lines, points, and dots on a piece of paper or another surface. The lines, points, and dots can be drawn in any order and with any amount of space between them. Once the lines, points, and dots have been drawn, they can be interpreted for their meaning.

When using this method, ensure that the lines, points, and dots are randomly placed. To personalize this method, you can use a randomly generated word or phrase as a guide for where to place the lines, points, and dots.

2. Throwing Dice

Dice can also be used to cast the points. This method involves rolling a pair of dice and using the numbers you get to determine where to place the lines, points, and dots. This can be done with two regular six-sided dice or with four special geomantic dice.

Throwing dice is sometimes used to cast the points.
https://pixabay.com/es/photos/costa-rica-dado-dice-dados-dices-4979191/

The color of the dice can also be used to add meaning to the figures that are created. White dice represent purity, while black dice represent darkness. Red dice represent passion, while blue dice represent calm. Green dice represent growth, while yellow dice represent wisdom.

To begin, the dice are thrown onto a flat surface. The dots on the dice represent the elements of fire, water, air, and earth. The total of the dots determines which element is being represented. For example, if the total is 12, then the element would be fire. Once the element has been determined, it can be entered into the chart.

The numbers on the dice can be interpreted in various ways, but one common method is to use the numbers as coordinates. This means that the first number rolled corresponds to the x-coordinate, and the second number rolled corresponds to the y-coordinate. This method of casting points is quick and easy; anyone can learn how to do it!

3. Flipping Coins

Flipping coins is another method for casting points.
https://unsplash.com/photos/b4D7FKAghoE?utm_source=unsplash&utm_medium=referral&utm_content=creditShareLink

Flipping coins is another popular method for casting points. This can be done with a regular coin, or you can use a special geomantic coin. Once you have your coin, you will need to decide how many points you want to cast. Each point represents a different aspect of your question, and the more points you cast, the more detailed your reading will be.

To cast your points, simply flip your coin onto the ground and observe which way it lands. Heads are considered positive, while tails are negative. You can interpret the results in various ways, but one common method is to use the positions of the coins to create a geomantic figure. This figure can then be interpreted for its meaning.

4. Using Geomancy Cards

Geomancy cards are a special deck of cards used for divination. Each card in the deck represents a different element, and the deck can be used to cast the points. To use the geomancy cards, simply shuffle the deck and lay out the cards in a row. The number of cards in your layout will depend on how many points you want to cast.

Once the cards are laid out, interpret their meaning based on the traditional meanings of the elements. For example, fire is associated with passion, while water is associated with emotions. Use the card positions to create a geomantic figure, and then interpret the figure for its meaning.

The printables at the end of this book can be used to create your geomantic cards. Simply print out the sheets, cut out the cards, and then shuffle them.

5. Casting the Points with a Pendulum

A pendulum can also be used to cast the points. This method involves holding a pendulum over a piece of paper or other surface and allowing it to swing freely. This method is quick and easy, and anyone can learn how to do it. The only downside is that it can be difficult to interpret the results. You can use various Pendulums for this method, but one common type is a quartz crystal Pendulum.

To use this method, simply hold the pendulum over the paper or surface. The pendulum will swing in a variety of directions. Take note of the direction it swings and the number of times it swings. This will give you the coordinates for where to place the lines, points, and dots. Once all of the coordinates have been determined, you can interpret the figure for its meaning.

6. Casting the Points with a Bowl of Water

The traditional way of casting points for geomantic readings is to use a bowl of water. The bowl is filled with water and placed on a table or other flat surface. The querent then stirs the water with their finger while concentrating on their question. After a minute or so of stirring the water, they remove their finger and look at the pattern made by the ripples.

The pattern interpretation is based on the specific shapes that are formed and the overall balance of positive and negative space. The space around the querent's finger is considered positive, while the space away from the finger is considered negative.

If there is more positive space, then the reading is considered favorable. However, the reading is interpreted as unfavorable if there is more negative space. This method is quick and easy, and anyone can learn how to do it.

7. Casting the Points with a Flame

Another traditional method for casting points is to use a flame. This method involves lighting a candle and then allowing the wax to drip into a bowl of water. The querent then concentrates on their question while the wax is melting. Once the wax has melted, the querent looks at the pattern that is formed and interprets it for its meaning.

This method is similar to the water method but uses a flame instead of water. The interpretation is based on the same principles, but using a flame can add an extra layer of meaning. For example, fire is associated with passion, so a reading that features a lot of fire energy may be interpreted as being passionate or intense.

The specific shapes formed by the wax can also be interpreted for their meaning. For instance, a heart shape may represent love, while a spiral shape may represent transformation. If you are using this method, it is crucial to be familiar with the traditional meanings of the shapes.

8. Casting the Points with Stones

Stones can also be used to cast the points. This method involves placing a stone on each of the geomantic figures. The querent then concentrates on their question while holding the stones. Based on the stones' positions, the querent can interpret the figure for its meaning. This method can be used with any type of stone, but some common choices include quartz crystals, amethysts, and rose quartz.

The stones can be placed on the figures in a variety of ways. The most common method is to place them in the center of each figure. However, they can also be placed on the lines that connect the figures. The interpretation will be based on the stones' positions and energies.

If you are using this method, selecting stones that are energetically compatible with the question you are asking is vital. For example, if you are asking a question about love, you would want to choose stones that are associated with love, such as rose quartz or amethyst.

9. Casting the Points Using Sticks

One of the simplest and most effective ways to cast points for a reading is to use sticks. First, find a clearing in nature where you will be undisturbed. Then, collect a bundle of small sticks and find a comfortable place to sit. Close your eyes and take a few deep breaths, letting go of all your worries and concerns.

Open your eyes and cast the sticks onto the ground when you are ready. The patterns that they make can be interpreted according to traditional geomantic meanings. For example, a row of four sticks pointing in the same direction may represent growth or new beginnings.

This method is great for connecting with nature and tapping into your intuition. It is also one of the easiest methods to learn since there is no need to memorize complex shapes or symbols. By taking the time to connect with the Earth through geomancy, you can gain valuable insights into your life journey.

10. Casting the Points with a Deck of Cards

You can also use a regular deck of playing cards to cast the points. This complex method requires knowledge of the traditional meanings of the geomantic figures. There are many different ways to do this, but one of the most common is to deal four cards for each figure.

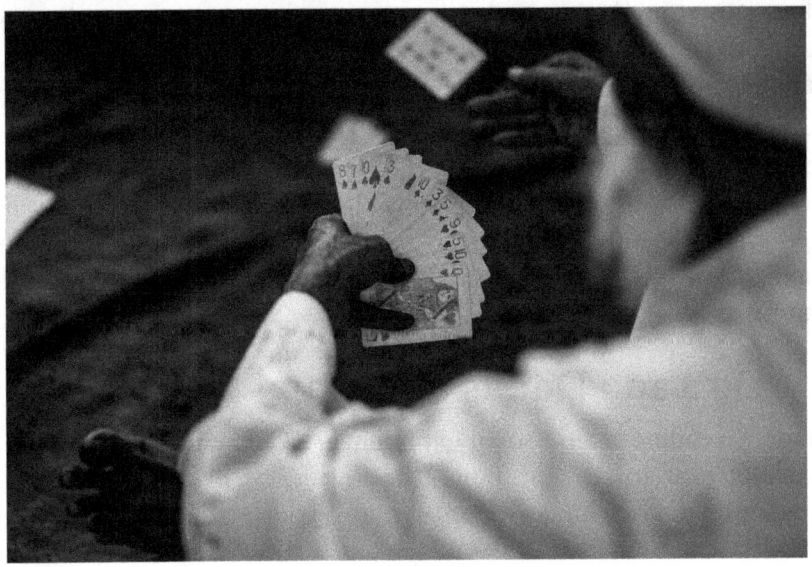

A basic set of playing cards can be used to cast points.
https://pixabay.com/es/photos/adulto-asia-tarjetas-divertida-3170055/

The specific position of the cards will determine the meaning of the figure. For example, if the first card is placed in the center of the figure, it will represent the querent. The other three cards will represent the influences of the past, present, and future.

To begin, shuffle the deck of cards and then deal out four cards face down. These four cards represent the four geomantic figures. Next, deal out four more cards and place them on top of the first four. Then, deal out four more cards and place them on top of the second set of four. The querent then asks their question.

The final step is to turn over the cards and interpret the figures based on the traditional meanings. This method can be quite complex, but it can be used for any question, especially for those relating to the querent's past, present, and future. By understanding the influences of each period, the querent can gain valuable insights into their life journey.

Personalizing the Method

While there are many ways to cast the points, the critical part is to find a method that works for you. If you are new to geomancy, it is best to start with a simple method and then build up to more complex ones. Some simple methods include using sticks or stones.

If you want to personalize the method, you can use objects that are significant to you. For example, if you are asking a question about your career, you could use coins or shells. The key is choosing objects that you feel comfortable with and that have personal meaning.

As you become more familiar with geomancy, you can experiment with different methods and techniques. You can move on to more complex methods, such as using a deck of cards. Or you can try different ways of interpreting the figures. There is no right or wrong way to do it. Finding a method that works for you and one you feel comfortable with is important.

Do's and Don'ts of Casting the Points

Geomantic reading is a personal experience, so there are no hard and fast rules about how to cast the points. However, there are a few things to remember to ensure you get the most out of your reading.

Do
- Find a quiet place where you will not be disturbed
- Relax and take a few deep breaths before you begin
- Choose a method you feel comfortable with
- Ask a specific question. The more specific the question, the more accurate the reading will be
- Be open to the answers you receive

Do Not
- Rush through the process
- Force the figures to fit your question
- Be afraid to ask tough questions

By following these simple guidelines, you can ensure that you get the most out of your geomantic reading. While these are just the basic things, here are some extra tips:

A. Asking the Question

The first step is to ask a specific question. The more specific the question, the more accurate the reading will be. First, make sure that the question is clear and specific. This will help focus the reading and produce more accurate results. Secondly, do not be too vague or open-ended. Asking a question like "What does my future hold?" is likely to produce very confusing results. ***Be as specific as possible.***

Finally, remember that the question should be framed in a way that can be answered with a yes or no. Asking a question like "Should I move to a new city?" will give you much more useful information than asking, "What are my options?" By following these simple guidelines, you can ensure that you get the most accurate reading possible from your geomantic points.

B. Avoiding Mistakes

There are a few common mistakes people make when doing geomancy readings. The first mistake that is made is rushing through the process. Secondly, they try to force the figures to fit their question. Thirdly, they are afraid to ask tough questions. By avoiding these mistakes, you can ensure that you get the most accurate reading possible.

If you find that you are making these mistakes, do not worry. Just take a step back and relax. Remember, there is no rush. Take your time and focus on your question. Then, let the figures fall where they may. The most important thing is to be open to the answers you receive.

C. Interpreting the Figures

Once you have cast the points, it is time to interpret the figures, and there are a few different ways to do this. First, you can look up the meaning of each figure in a book or online. Second, you can ask someone else to interpret the figures for you. Finally, you can interpret the figures yourself.

If you choose to interpret the figures yourself, there are a few things to keep in mind. First, trust your intuition. Second, look at the overall pattern of the figures. Third, pay attention to any recurring themes. By following these simple guidelines, you can ensure that you get the most accurate reading possible.

D. Other Tips and Advice

Here are a few other tips and pieces of advice to keep in mind when doing geomancy readings.

- Do not be afraid to experiment. There is no one right way.
- Do not be afraid to ask tough questions and be open to the answers you receive.
- Trust your intuition and keep an open mind.
- Keep a journal of your readings. This will help you track your progress and see how your skills develop over time.
- Do not take the readings too seriously. Remember, they are just a tool to help you gain insights into your life. They are not always 100% accurate.
- Geomancy is a great way to connect with your intuition and gain insights into your life. Enjoy the process and see what insights you can glean from it.

Casting the points is the first step in doing a geomancy reading. This chapter discussed the various methods of casting the points, as well as how to avoid common mistakes. For beginners, it is recommended to use the traditional methods of casting the points using colored dice, sticks, or coins.

When you are confident with your skills, you can start to experiment with other methods of casting the points. It is important to be specific in your question, open to the answers you receive, and avoid mistakes such as rushing through the process.

After casting the points, you can then interpret the figures. There are a few different ways to interpret the figures, including looking up the meaning of each figure, asking someone else to interpret the figures, or interpreting the figures yourself. The next chapter will discuss how to interpret the figures in more detail.

So, there you have it, a complete guide on how to cast the points for a geomancy reading. By following these simple tips, you can ensure that you get the most accurate reading possible.

Chapter 7: The Geomantic Figures

Can the same be said about geomantic figures? What do they mean, and is there more than one way to interpret them?

Once you have learned how to cast the points and create the geomantic figures, you will want to understand their meaning. The symbols used in geomancy are based on ancient ideas about the four elements, the planets, and the zodiac.

Each figure has its meaning, and you can gain insights into your own life and situation by interpreting the figures. In addition, geomancy can be used for divination or predicting the future. By asking a question and casting the points, you can receive guidance from the geomantic figures.

With practice, you will develop your ability to interpret the symbols and use them to gain insights into your life path. This chapter will provide an introduction to the meanings of the geomantic figures.

Decrypting Geomantic Figures

Geomantic figures are created by making marks in the sand or dirt. The number of marks and the way they are arranged all have meaning. For example, a figure with four marks arranged in a cross shape indicates that the person is feeling balanced and stable. A figure with eight marks arranged in a circle indicates that the person is feeling connected to their surroundings.

We can learn a lot about individuals' inner lives by decoding the meaning of these graphs. In some cultures, geomantic figures are used for divination to help people make decisions about their future. In other cultures, they are used as part of healing rituals, providing a way for people to express their fears and anxieties. Regardless of how they are used, geomantic figures offer a valuable window into the human soul.

What They Mean

Geomantic figures can be divided into two groups. The first group includes the four elemental figures, representing matter's fundamental building blocks. The second group includes the twelve zodiacal figures, representing the energies that shape our lives.

Geomancy uses the arrangement of 16 figures, each composed of four points. Of these, eight are considered "positive" or "active," and the other eight are "negative" or "passive." The active figures are those in which the first and third points are both marked, while the passive figures are those in which only the second and fourth points are marked.

The eight active figures are called "masculine," while the eight passive figures are called "feminine." The masculine figures represent the Yang energy, while the feminine figures represent the Yin energy. These energies are believed to be in constant interaction, and the interplay between them creates the universe's harmony.

The Connection between Figures

Here are some things that connect the four types of geomantic figures:

1. Elements

There are four main types of geomantic figures, water, fire, earth, and air. Each type has its unique characteristics, but they also have some things in common. All four types of figures are associated with a specific element. Water figures are associated with the element of water, fire figures with the element of fire, earth figures with the element of earth, and air figures with the element of air.

2. Zodiac Signs

The 12 zodiac figures are each associated with a specific zodiac sign. Water signs are associated with the signs of Cancer, Scorpio, fire signs are associated with the signs of Aries, Leo, and Sagittarius, earth signs are associated with the signs of Taurus, Virgo, and Capricorn, and air signs are associated with the signs of Gemini, Libra, and Aquarius.

3. Planets

All four types of figures are connected to a specific planet. Water figures are connected to the planet Mercury, fire figures are connected to the planet Mars, earth figures are connected to the planet Saturn, and air figures are connected to the planet Jupiter. The connection between planets and geomantic figures can help us understand these astronomical bodies' influence on our lives.

4. Divination

Finally, all four types of figures have a specific role in divination. Water figures represent emotions and intuition, fire figures represent passion and energy, earth figures represent stability and structure, and air figures represent intellect and wisdom. By understanding these commonalities, you can begin to see how each type of figure is related to the others.

Understanding the Properties of the Figures

If you want to learn more about the geomantic figures, it is crucial to understand the properties of each type. Here is a brief overview of the properties of geomantic figures:

1. **Quality:** A figure can be stable or mobile. A stable figure does not change, while a mobile figure is in flux. The stability or mobility of a figure reflects the quality of the energy it represents.

2. **Direction:** A figure can be entering, exiting, or both. An entering figure is one that is moving towards something, while an existing figure is one that is moving away from something. The direction of a figure reflects the flow of energy it represents.

3. **Humor:** A figure can be sanguine, choleric, melancholy, and phlegmatic. Sanguine humor is associated with positive emotions like happiness and optimism, choleric humor with negative emotions like anger and frustration, melancholy humor with introspection and contemplation, and phlegmatic humor with apathy and indifference.

4. **A Measure of Time:** A figure can be associated with a specific moment in time. The time associated with a figure reflects the duration of the energy it represents. The longer the time frame, the more significant the figure.

5. **Partiality:** A figure can be partial or impartial. A partial figure is one that applies to a specific situation, while an impartial figure is one

that can be applied to any situation. The partiality of a figure reflects the specific nature of the energy it represents.

By understanding the properties of geomantic figures, you can begin to see how they can be used in divination.

Interpreting the Figures

Now that you have a basic understanding of the geomantic figures, it is time to learn how to interpret them. When interpreting the figures, it is crucial to keep the following guidelines in mind:

1. **The Position of the Figure in Relation to the Others**: The position of a figure can tell you a lot about its meaning. For example, a figure in the center of the chart is considered to be more important than the ones on the periphery.

2. **The Orientation of the Figure:** The orientation of a figure can also be important. An upright figure is considered more positive than a reversed one.

3. **The Type of Figure:** The type of figure can help understand its meaning. For example, a water figure is typically associated with emotions, while a fire figure is typically associated with passion.

4. **The Planet Associated with the Figure:** The planet associated with a figure can also help you understand its meaning. For example, a figure associated with the planet Mercury is typically associated with communication and commerce.

The General Meaning of Each Figure

Now that you know how to interpret the figures, it is time to learn about their meanings. Here is a brief overview of the general meaning of each figure:

Tristitia

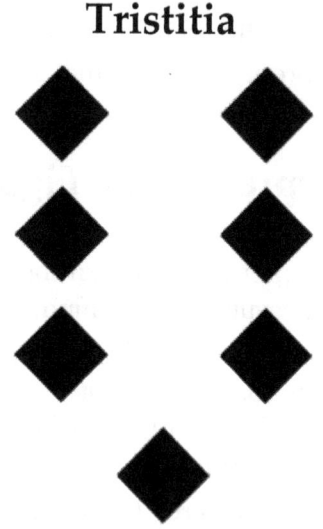

Trisitia.
https://commons.wikimedia.org/wiki/File:Geomantic_tristitia.svg

Translation: Sorrow
Keywords: Loss, Grief, Sadness, Depression
Ruling Element: Earth
Ruling Planet: Saturn
Ruling Zodiac Sign: Aquarius
Quality: Stable
Direction: Entering
Partial/Impartial: Partial
Diurnal/Nocturnal: Diurnal

Tristitia is a figure associated with loss and grief. It can represent a sad or depressing situation. It can also indicate a period of transition or change. This figure is typically associated with the planet Saturn and the zodiac sign Aquarius. The quality of Tristitia is stable, which represents the constancy of emotions like sadness and grief.

The direction of this figure is entering, which means that it is moving towards something. This could represent the beginning of a period of grief or the start of a new chapter in life. The partiality of this figure indicates that it only applies to specific situations. This figure is diurnal, which means that it is active during the day.

Puer

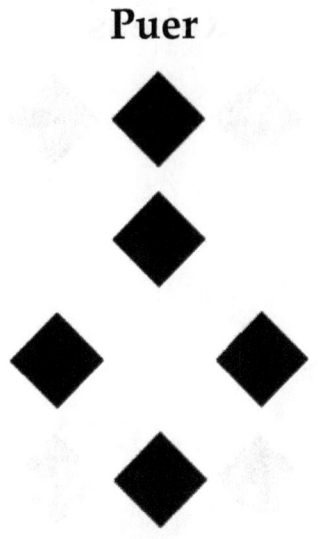

Puer.
https://commons.wikimedia.org/wiki/File:Geomantic_puer.svg

Translation: Boy
Keywords: Youth, Innocence, Beginnings
Ruling Element: Air
Ruling Planet: Mars
Ruling Zodiac Sign: Aries
Quality: Mobile
Direction: Exiting
Partial/Impartial: Partial
Diurnal/Nocturnal: Diurnal

Puer is a figure associated with youth and innocence. It can represent the beginning of a new project or venture. It can also indicate a time of growth or expansion. This figure is typically associated with the planet Mars and the zodiac sign Aries. The quality of Puer is mobile, which represents the energy and activity of youth.

The direction of this figure is exiting, which means it is moving away from something. This could represent the end of a project or the completion of a phase of growth. The partiality of this figure indicates that it only applies to specific situations. This figure is diurnal, which means that it is active during the day.

Rubeus

Rubeus.
https://commons.wikimedia.org/wiki/File:Geomantic_rubeus.svg

Translation: Red
Keywords: Anger, Aggression, Violence, Passion
Ruling Element: Air
Ruling Planet: Mars
Ruling Zodiac Sign: Scorpio
Quality: Mobile
Direction: Exiting
Partial/Impartial: Partial
Diurnal/Nocturnal: Nocturnal

Rubeus is a figure associated with anger and aggression. It can represent a violent or passionate situation. It can also indicate a time of upheaval or change. This figure is typically associated with the planet Mars and the zodiac sign Scorpio. The quality of Rubeus is mobile, which represents the energy and activity of anger.

The direction of this figure is exiting, which means it is moving away from something. This could represent the end of a situation or the completion of a phase of change. The partiality of this figure indicates that it only applies to specific situations. This figure is nocturnal, which means it is active during the night.

Caput Draconis

Caput draconis.
https://commons.wikimedia.org/wiki/File:Geomantic_caputdraconis.svg

Translation: Dragon's Head
Keywords: Transformation, New Beginnings, Metamorphosis
Ruling Element: Earth
Ruling Planet: Moon's North Node
Ruling Zodiac Sign: Pisces
Quality: Stable
Direction: Entering
Partial/Impartial: Partial
Diurnal/Nocturnal: Diurnal

Caput Draconis is a figure associated with transformation and new beginnings. It can represent a changing or evolving situation. It can also indicate a time of growth or expansion. This figure is typically associated with the Lunar Nodes and the zodiac sign Pisces. The quality of Caput Draconis is stable, which represents the constancy of change.

The direction of this figure is entering, which means it is moving towards something. This could represent the beginning of a new phase or the start of a new chapter in life. The partiality of this figure indicates that it only applies to specific situations. This figure is diurnal, which means it is active during the day.

Cauda Draconis

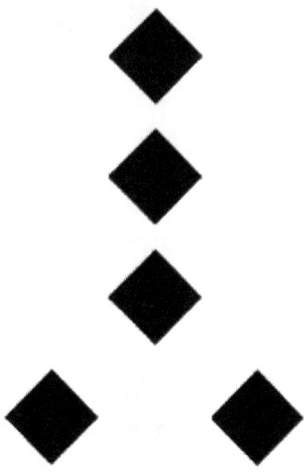

Cauda Draconis.
https://commons.wikimedia.org/wiki/File:Geomantic_caudadraconis.svg

Translation: Dragon's Tail
Keywords: Endings, Completion, Death
Ruling Element: Fire
Ruling Planet: Moon's South Node
Ruling Zodiac Sign: Virgo
Quality: Mobile
Direction: Exiting
Partial/Impartial: Partial
Diurnal/Nocturnal: Nocturnal

Cauda Draconis is a figure associated with endings and completion. It can also represent death, but that is not always the case. The fire element rules this figure which represents passion and intensity. The planet associated with Cauda Draconis is the Moon's South Node, which is a point of karma and destiny.

The ruling zodiac sign is Virgo, an earth sign associated with service and practicality. This figure is mobile, meaning that it is constantly changing and is never in one place for long. It is also partial, which means that it is not complete and always has the potential to change. Cauda Draconis is a nocturnal figure, meaning that it is most powerful at night.

Puella

Puella.
https://commons.wikimedia.org/wiki/File:Geomantic_puella.svg

Translation: Girl
Keywords: Youth, Innocence, Beginnings
Ruling Element: Water
Ruling Planet: Venus
Ruling Zodiac Sign: Libra
Quality: Stable
Direction: Entering
Partial/Impartial: Partial
Diurnal/Nocturnal: Diurnal

Puella is a figure that represents youth and innocence. It can also signify beginnings, as it is associated with the water element, which is representative of new beginnings. The planet Venus rules this figure, which is associated with love, beauty, and femininity. The zodiac sign Libra is also ruled by Venus and is symbolized by the scales of justice.

Puella is a stable figure, meaning that it does not change much over time. It is also partial, indicating that there is always room for growth and development. This figure is diurnal, meaning that it is most powerful during the day.

Conjunctio

Conjunctio.
https://commons.wikimedia.org/wiki/File:Geomantic_conjunctio.svg

Translation: Union
Keywords: Partnership, Cooperation, Balance
Ruling Element: Air
Ruling Planet: Mercury
Ruling Zodiac Sign: Gemini
Quality: Mobile
Direction: Both
Partial/Impartial: Impartial
Diurnal/Nocturnal: Nocturnal

Conjunctio is a figure that represents partnership and cooperation. It is also associated with the air element, which signifies balance. The planet Mercury rules this figure, which is associated with communication and commerce. This figure is mobile, meaning that it is constantly changing and never in one place for long. It is also impartial, which means that it does not favor one side over the other. Conjunctio is a nocturnal figure, meaning that it is most powerful at night.

Albus

Albus.
https://commons.wikimedia.org/wiki/File:Geomantic_albus.svg

Translation: White
Keywords: Purity, Hope, New Beginnings
Ruling Element: Water
Ruling Planet: Mercury
Ruling Zodiac Sign: Gemini
Quality: Stable
Direction: Entering
Partial/Impartial: Partial
Diurnal/Nocturnal: Diurnal

Albus is a figure that represents purity and hope. It is also associated with the water element, which signifies new beginnings. The planet Mercury rules this figure, which is associated with communication and commerce. This figure is stable, meaning that it does not change much over time. It is also partial, indicating that there is always room for growth and development. Albus is a diurnal figure, meaning that it is most powerful during the day.

Via

Via.
https://commons.wikimedia.org/wiki/File:Geomantic_via.svg

Translation: Road
Keywords: Journey, Change, Movement
Ruling Element: Earth
Ruling Planet: Moon
Ruling Zodiac Sign: Cancer
Quality: Mobile
Direction: Both
Partial/Impartial: Impartial
Diurnal/Nocturnal: Nocturnal

Via is a figure that represents journey and change. It is also associated with the earth element, which signifies stability. The planet Moon rules this figure, which is associated with emotions and intuition. This figure is mobile, meaning that it is constantly changing and never in one place for long. It is also impartial, which means that it does not favor one side over the other. Via is a nocturnal figure, meaning that it is most powerful at night.

Populus

Populus.
https://commons.wikimedia.org/wiki/File:Geomantic_populus.svg

Translation: People
Keywords: Community, Society, Relationship
Ruling Element: Water
Ruling Planet: Moon
Ruling Zodiac Sign: Aquarius
Quality: Stable
Direction: Both
Partial/Impartial: Impartial
Diurnal/Nocturnal: Diurnal

Populus is a figure that represents community and society. It is also associated with the water element, which signifies relationships. The planet Moon rules this figure, which is associated with emotions and intuition. This figure is stable, meaning that it does not change much over time. It is also impartial, which means that it does not favor one side over the other. Populus is a diurnal figure, meaning that it is at its most powerful during the day.

Fortuna Minor

Fortuna minor.
https://commons.wikimedia.org/wiki/File:Geomantic_fortunaminor.svg

Translation: Lesser Fortune
Keywords: Opportunity, Good Luck, Progress
Ruling Element: Fire
Ruling Planet: Sun
Ruling Zodiac Sign: Leo
Quality: Mobile
Direction: Exiting
Partial/Impartial: Impartial
Diurnal/Nocturnal: Diurnal

Fortuna Minor is a figure that represents opportunity and good luck. It is also associated with the fire element, which signifies progress. The planet Sun rules this figure, which is associated with vitality and life force. This figure is mobile, meaning it is constantly changing and never in one place for long. It is also impartial, which means that it does not favor one side over the other. Fortuna Minor is a diurnal figure, meaning that it is most powerful during the day.

Acquisitio

Acquisito.
https://commons.wikimedia.org/wiki/File:Geomantic_acquisitio.svg

Translation: Acquisition
Keywords: Gain, Profit, Success
Ruling Element: Air
Ruling Planet: Jupiter
Ruling Zodiac Sign: Sagittarius
Quality: Stable
Direction: Entering
Partial/Impartial: Impartial
Diurnal/Nocturnal: Diurnal

Acquisitio is a figure that represents gain and success. It is also associated with the air element, which signifies expansion. The planet Jupiter rules this figure, which is associated with abundance and prosperity. This figure is stable, meaning that it does not change much over time. It is also impartial, which means that it does not favor one side over the other. Acquisitio is a diurnal figure, meaning that it is most powerful during the day.

Amissio

Amissio.
https://commons.wikimedia.org/wiki/File:Geomantic_amissio.svg

Translation: Loss
Keywords: Defeat, Setback, Failure
Ruling Element: Fire
Ruling Planet: Venus
Ruling Zodiac Sign: Capricorn
Quality: Mobile
Direction: Exiting
Partial/Impartial: Impartial
Diurnal/Nocturnal: Nocturnal

Amissio is a figure that represents loss and failure. It is also associated with the fire element, which signifies destruction. The planet Venus rules this figure, which is associated with love and beauty. This figure is mobile, meaning that it is constantly changing and never in one place for long. It is also impartial, which means that it does not favor one side over the other. Amissio is a nocturnal figure, meaning that it is most powerful at night.

Cancer

Translation: Prison
Keywords: Restriction, Delay, Frustration
Ruling Element: Earth
Ruling Planet: Saturn
Ruling Zodiac Sign: Capricorn
Quality: Stable
Direction: Both
Partial/Impartial: Impartial
Diurnal/Nocturnal: Nocturnal

Carcer is a figure that represents restriction and delay. It is also associated with the earth element, which signifies stability. The planet Saturn rules this figure, which is associated with limitations and boundaries. This figure is stable, meaning that it does not change much over time. It is also impartial, which means that it does not favor one side over the other. Carcer is a nocturnal figure, meaning that it is most powerful at night.

Fortuna Major

Fortuna major.
https://commons.wikimedia.org/wiki/File:Geomantic_fortunamajor.svg

Translation: Greater Fortune
Keywords: Good Luck, Success, Progress
Ruling Element: Earth
Ruling Planet: Sun
Ruling Zodiac Sign: Leo
Quality: Stable
Direction: Entering
Partial/Impartial: Impartial
Diurnal/Nocturnal: Nocturnal

Fortuna Major is a figure that represents good luck and success. It is also associated with the earth element, which signifies grounding. The planet Sun rules this figure, which is associated with vitality and life force. This figure is stable, meaning that it does not change much over time. It is also impartial, which means that it does not favor one side over the other. Fortuna Major is a nocturnal figure, meaning that it is most powerful at night.

Laetitia

Laetitia.
https://commons.wikimedia.org/wiki/File:Geomantic_laetitia.svg

Translation: Joy
Keywords: Happiness, Celebration, Triumph
Ruling Element: Fire
Ruling Planet: Jupiter
Ruling Zodiac Sign: Pisces
Quality: Mobile
Direction: Exiting
Partial/Impartial: Partial
Diurnal/Nocturnal: Nocturnal

Laetitia is a figure that represents happiness and celebration. It is also associated with the fire element, which signifies passion. The planet Jupiter rules this figure, which is associated with luck and opportunity. This figure is mobile, meaning that it is constantly changing and never in one place for long. It is also partial, which means that it favors one side over the other. Laetitia is a nocturnal figure, meaning that it is most powerful at night.

Interpreting the Geomantic Figures can give you a greater understanding of the energies at play in your life. They can also help you make decisions by providing guidance and insight. To learn more about the Geomantic Figures, consult a professional astrologer or tarot reader.

This chapter only scratches the surface of this complex and fascinating topic.

Note: No figure is purely negative, and the reader should not perceive any figure as a bad omen.

Chapter 8: Constructing a Shield Chart

Do you easily see signs and understand them? Do you feel as if you have a strong connection to the spiritual world? If your answer is yes, then it is time for you to start learning how to practice geomancy. Once you have cast your geomantic figures, it is time to construct a shield chart to start the interpretation process.

The shield chart is the main structure through which you can do a geomantic reading. This step is vital to understanding the message your figures are trying to tell you. In this chapter, we will discuss the shield chart in detail, including its segments and what each of them represents. By the end of this chapter, you will know how to construct your shield chart and interpret its message.

The Geomantic Shield Chart

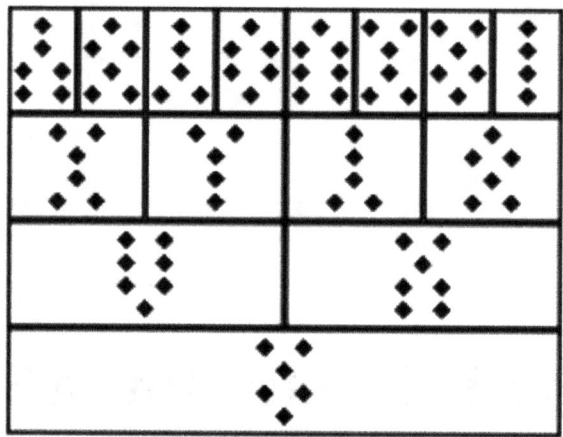

The geomantic shield chart.
https://commons.wikimedia.org/wiki/File:Geomantic_shieldchart.svg

The geomantic shield is the primary tool used to interpret a geomantic reading. The shield chart is made up of 16 house segments, each of which corresponds to a specific geomantic figure. These house segments are further divided into 4 groups of 4 houses each, called quadrants. The quadrants are used to delineate the different areas of a person's life that the reading may be touching on.

The shield chart is read from the bottom up. The first quadrant, which is the bottommost one, corresponds to the most recent past. The second quadrant corresponds to the near future. The third quadrant corresponds to the distant future, and the fourth quadrant, the topmost one, corresponds to the outcome.

The quadrants are not equal in size, nor are the house segments within each quadrant. The size and placement of the quadrants and house segments are all determined by the specific question you are asking or the topic of your reading. The shield chart can be used for a variety of purposes, such as answering specific questions, doing general readings, or understanding the energy of a particular situation.

The Origins of the Geomantic Shield Chart

The origins of the shield chart are unknown, but it is believed to have originated in the Arab world. The earliest known mention of the shield chart is in Fate of the Universe by Abu al-Rayhan al-Biruni. In this book,

Biruni describes a shield chart that is used to predict future events.

This book includes a description of how to construct a shield chart and the meaning of each quadrant and house segment. It is believed that the shield chart was later adopted by European geomancers, who added their twists and modifications.

Some people believe that the geomantic shield chart originated in China, where it was used as a tool for divination. Feng Shui practitioners believe that the chart can be used to identify areas of imbalance in a space and to make recommendations for correcting those imbalances.

The use of the geomantic shield chart has spread to other parts of Asia and has also gained popularity in the West. Today, there are many different versions of the chart, each of which has its unique symbols and meaning. In the next section, we will take a closer look at the function of the geomantic shield chart.

The Function of the Geomantic Shield Chart

A geomantic shield chart is a tool used by Feng Shui practitioners to evaluate the energy of a space. The shield chart is used to interpret the message of the geomantic figures. The figure that falls in each housing segment can give you information about the past, present, and future. When you are doing a reading for yourself, you will need to construct your geomantic shield chart.

To help you better understand the shield chart, here are some of its functions:

- The geomantic shield chart can be used to answer specific questions
- It can be used to get a general overview of a situation
- It can be used to understand the energy of a particular situation
- It can be used to make recommendations for improving the energy of a space
- It can be used to find areas of imbalance in a space
- It can be used to understand the dynamics of a relationship
- It can be used to make predictions

Having a better understanding of the geomantic shield chart will help you to use it more effectively. In the next section, we will take a closer look at the segments of a geomantic shield chart.

The Segments of the Geomantic Shield Chart

The geomantic shield chart is composed of four segments, each representing a different stage in the reading process. The first segment, known as the Mothers, is used to identify the potential influences on a given situation. The second segment, the Daughters, is used to further refine the reading by considering the nature of the influences at play.

The third segment, the Witnesses, is used to weigh the evidence and determine which course of action is best. Finally, the fourth segment, the Judge, is used to pronounce a verdict based on the findings of the previous three segments. By carefully considering all four segments, practitioners can gain a deeper understanding of the complex interplay between human and natural forces.

The following section will provide you with a more detailed look at each of the segments in a geomantic shield chart.

A. The Mothers

Description: The first segment of the chart, known as the Mothers, is used to identify the potential influences on a given situation. This segment is divided into four quadrants, each of which is ruled by a different Mother. These Mothers represent the four elements of fire, earth, air, and water.

Each Mother has a unique symbol and meaning. The Mothers can be used to understand the energy of a space and to make recommendations for improving the balance of that space. The Mothers are the fundamental forces at work in any given situation, and they can be either positive or negative.

Meaning: The Mothers represent the building blocks of reading, and they can be thought of as the foundation upon which the rest of the chart is built. The Mothers provide the reader with a starting point from which they can understand the situation at hand. The first step in any reading is to identify the Mother that is most relevant to the question at hand.

This Mother will provide the reader with an initial understanding of the situation and will give them a general idea of what to expect. From there, the reader can begin to refine their understanding by considering the other Mothers.

What Each Figure Transmits in a Reading

When a geomantic figure is sitting in the Mother's shield segment, it is transmitting a very important message. For example, if the figure is 'Puella,' then it is transmitting a message of purity, innocence, and new beginnings. If the figure is 'Populus,' then it is transmitting a message of community, cooperation, and compromise.

Similarly, Fortuna Major is associated with good fortune, luck, and opportunity. When sitting in the Mother's shield segment, it can indicate that the situation is favorable. Via is associated with passion, enthusiasm, and energy. When used within the Mother's shield segment, it can indicate that the issue at hand is of great importance.

The Mothers segment of the chart is used to identify the potential influences on a given situation.

B. The Daughters

Description: The second segment of the chart, known as the Daughters, is used to further refine the reading by considering the nature of the influences at play. This segment is divided into four quadrants, each of which is ruled by a different Daughter. These Daughters represent the four suits of the tarot, cups, swords, wands, and pentacles.

Each Daughter has a unique symbol and meaning. The Daughters can be used to understand the dynamics of a situation and to make recommendations for how to best navigate that situation. The Daughters are the more specific forces at work in any given situation, and they can be either positive or negative.

Meaning: The Daughters provide the reader with a more specific understanding of the situation at hand. The second step in any reading is to identify the Daughter that is most relevant to the question at hand. This Daughter will provide the reader with an idea of what to expect. From there, the reader can begin to refine their understanding by considering the other Daughters.

What Each Figure Transmits in a Reading

When a geomantic figure is sitting in the Daughter's shield segment, it means that the figure is specifically transmitting a message about that suit. For example, if the figure is 'Rubeus,' then it is transmitting a message about the suit of wands (fire). This message could be interpreted to mean that the situation is dangerous or that caution should be exercised.

If the figure is 'Cauda Draconis,' then it is transmitting a message about the suit of swords (air). This message could be interpreted to mean that the situation is confused or that there is a need for clarification. The Daughters segment of the chart is used to understand the specific influences at work in any given situation.

C. The Witnesses

Description: The third segment of the chart, known as the Witnesses, is used to further refine the reading by considering the role that other people play in the situation. This segment is divided into four quadrants, each of which is ruled by a different Witness. These Witnesses represent the four elements: fire, air, water, and earth.

Each Witness has its unique symbol and meaning. The Witnesses can be used to understand the dynamics of a situation and to make recommendations for how to best navigate that situation. The Witnesses are the people or factors that are not directly involved in the situation, but that can still have an impact on it.

Meaning: The Witnesses provide the reader with a more specific understanding of the situation at hand. The third step in any reading is to identify the Witness that is most relevant to the question at hand. This Witness will provide the reader with an idea of what to expect. From there, the reader can begin to refine their understanding by considering the other Witnesses.

What Each Figure Transmits in a Reading

When a geomantic figure is sitting in the Witness's shield segment, it means that the figure is specifically transmitting a message about that element. For example, if the figure is 'Albus,' then it is transmitting a message about the element of water. This message could be interpreted to mean that the situation is emotional or that there is a need for sensitivity.

If the figure is 'Populus,' then it is transmitting a message about the element of earth. This message could be interpreted to mean that the situation is materialistic or that there is a need for practicality. The Witnesses segment of the chart is used to understand the people or factors that are not directly involved in the situation, but that can still have an impact on it.

D. The Judge

Description: The fourth and final segment of the chart is known as the Judge. This segment is used to determine the outcome of the reading. The

Judge is represented by a single geomantic figure, which is placed in the center of the chart. This figure is known as the 'Judge' because it represents the final decision that will be made in the situation.

The Judge is not influenced by the other segments of the chart; instead, its determination is based on the position of the planets and the stars. The Judge is considered impartial and objective, and as such, their decision is final.

Meaning: The Judge provides the reader with a definitive understanding of the outcome of the situation. The fourth and final step in any reading is to identify the Judge. This graph will tell the reader what to anticipate. The Judge is not influenced by the other segments of the chart but makes its determination based on the position of the planets and the stars.

What Each Figure Transmits in a Reading

When a geomantic figure is sitting in the Judge's shield segment, it means that the figure is specifically transmitting a message about that planet or star. For example, if the figure is 'Fortuna Major,' then it is transmitting a message about the planet Jupiter. This message could be interpreted to mean that the situation will have a positive outcome.

If the figure is 'Via,' then it is transmitting a message about the star Saturn. This message could be interpreted to mean that the situation will have a negative or difficult outcome. The Judge segment of the chart is used to determine the outcome of the reading.

Constructing Your Shield Chart

When constructing a geomancy shield chart, the first step is to identify the question you want to be answered. Once you have done this, you will need to select a location for the chart. The chart can be drawn on any surface, but it is recommended that you use a piece of paper or cloth.

The next step is to identify the Shield Figures that you will use in your chart. There are a total of 16 Shield Figures, and each one represents a different element. You can choose to use all 16 figures, or you can select a smaller number. It is recommended that you select at least 8 figures.

Once you have selected your Shield Figures, you will need to place them in the appropriate segments of the chart. The Shield Figures are placed in the following order:

1. The Significator
2. The Mother
3. The Father
4. The Left Witness
5. The Right Witness
6. The Judge

Once you have placed all of the Shield Figures in their proper positions, you will need to draw lines connecting them. These lines are known as 'shield lines,' and they serve to create a connection between the figures.

Once you have drawn all of the shield lines, you will need to interpret the chart. The interpretation of the chart will depend on the question that you have asked, as well as the Shield Figures that you have used.

Putting It into Practice: Printable Shields

Now that you know how to construct a geomancy shield chart, you can put your knowledge into practice. At the end of the book are printable shields you can use for your readings. Use these shields to answer a question you have, and see what the outcome will be.

This chapter has provided you with a detailed explanation of how to construct a geomancy shield chart. You have also learned how to interpret the results of your chart. Constructing one is a simple process that anyone can do. All you need is a question, a location, and 16 Shield Figures. Once you have these things, you can construct your chart and begin to interpret the results. Try it for yourself and see what the future has in store for you.

Chapter 9: Generating an Astrological Chart

Do you know what your astrological chart looks like? If not, do not worry! In this chapter, we will show you how to generate an astrological chart so that you can begin to understand the role that astrology plays in your life. Geomancy and astrology are inextricably linked. A deep understanding of one will enhance your understanding of the other.

This chapter will explore how to use and interpret the second most common chart used by geomancers, the astrological chart. We will go through each house and explain what changed and the specific meaning each geomantic figure might transmit if situated in each of the astrological houses. But first, we need to understand what an astrological chart is.

Astrological Charts

An astrological chart is a snapshot of the sky at the moment you were born. It shows the position of the planets at that moment, as well as the signs of the zodiac in which they appear. An astrological chart is a two-dimensional map of the heavens at a specific moment in time. It is composed of twelve houses, each representing a different area of life experience, and ten planets, each representing different astrological energy.

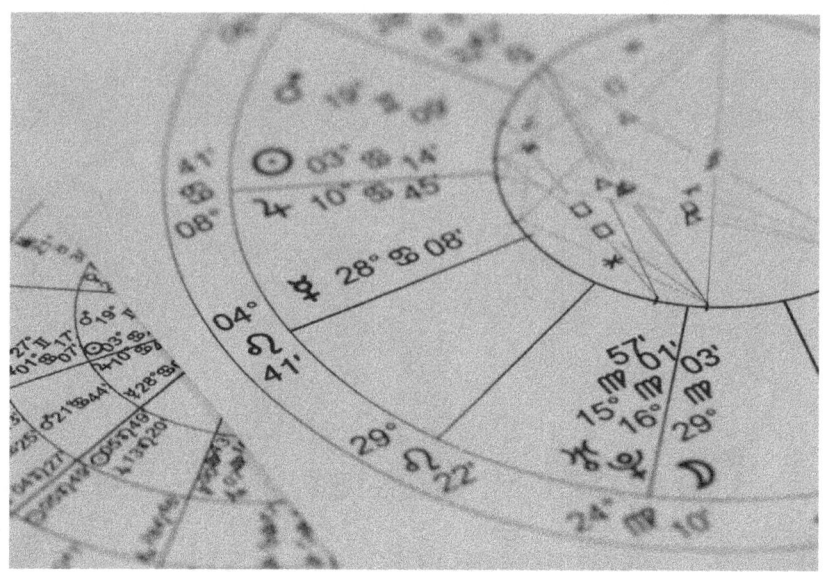

Astrological chart.
CC0 Public Domain https://pxhere.com/en/photo/682841

In addition, the chart includes the two nodes of the Moon, Rahu and Ketu, as well as the four angles of the chart, the Ascendant, Descendant, Midheaven, and IC (or Imum Coeli). These are the most important points in the chart, as they indicate the beginning, ending, highest point, and lowest point of your journey through life, respectively.

Planets in an Astrological Chart

The planets in an astrological chart are Sun, Moon, Mercury, Venus, Mars, Jupiter, Saturn, Uranus, Neptune, and Pluto. Each planet represents a different type of energy, which manifests in different ways in our lives. The Sun, for example, represents our ego and our sense of self. The Moon represents our emotions and our subconscious mind.

Mercury represents our communication style, and Venus represents our values and what we find beautiful. Mars represents our drive and ambition, and Jupiter represents our luck and expansion. Saturn represents our lessons and limitations, and Uranus represents our freedom and individuality. Neptune represents our spirituality and connection to the divine, and Pluto represents our power and transformation.

The Astrological Houses

The twelve houses of the astrological chart represent different areas of life experience. A geomantic figure situated in a particular house will have a different meaning than if it were in another house. Based on the planet that rules the house and the sign that occupies the said house, its meaning will change.

Understanding the meaning of the astrological houses is essential to understanding the role astrology plays in your life. This section will provide an overview of how a geomantic figure might be interpreted if situated in each of the twelve houses.

House of Self

Keywords: Self-identity, physical appearance, first impressions

The geomantic figure in the 1st House has a strong influence on your outward appearance and how you are seen by others. This figure is associated with your physical body and how you present yourself to the world. It also relates to your overall health and well-being.

If the figure is well-aspected, it indicates that you are likely both physically healthy and appealing. If the figure is poorly-aspected, it suggests that you may have physical health problems or an unattractive appearance. Whether well or poorly aspected, the 1st House figure is an important indicator of how you will be perceived by others.

When interpreting a figure in the 1st House, it is important to pay attention to the element and quality of the figure, as well as the planet that rules it. This will give you clues as to how the figure will manifest in your appearance and health.

For example, a Fire element figure in the 1st House indicates that you likely have a fiery personality and that you are very self-assertive. A Water element figure in the 1st House suggests that you are likely emotionally sensitive and that you have a compassionate nature.

House of Possessions

The geomantic figure in the 2nd House has a strong influence on your material possessions and your financial wellbeing. This figure is associated with your income, possessions, and values. It also relates to your self-esteem and your sense of self-worth.

If the figure is well-aspected, it indicates that you are likely financially successful and that you have high self-esteem. If the figure is poorly-aspected, it suggests that you may have financial problems or low self-esteem. Either way, the 2nd House figure is an important indicator of your relationship with money and possessions.

When interpreting a figure in the 2nd House, it is important to pay attention to the element and quality of the figure, as well as the planet that rules it. This will give you clues as to how the figure will manifest in your finances and possessions.

For example, a Fire element figure in the 2nd House indicates that you are likely generous with your money and possessions. A Water element figure in the 2nd House suggests that you are likely stingy with your money and possessions.

House of Communications

The geomantic figure in the 3rd House has a strong influence on your communication style and your ability to express yourself. This figure is associated with your verbal and written communication, as well as your ability to think clearly and reason logically. It also relates to your mental health and overall state of mind.

If the figure is well-aspected, it indicates that you are likely to articulate and that you have a sharp mind. If the figure is poorly-aspected, it suggests that you may have communication problems or mental health issues. Either way, the 3rd House figure is an important indicator of your ability to express yourself and engage in intellectual pursuits.

When interpreting a figure in the 3rd House, it is important to pay attention to the element and quality of the figure, as well as the planet that rules it. This will give you clues as to how the figure will manifest in your communication and thought processes. For example, a Fire element figure in the 3rd House indicates that you are likely expressive and enthusiastic when communicating. A Water element figure in the 3rd House suggests that you are likely introspective and compassionate when you are communicating.

House of Home and Family

The geomantic figure in the 4th House strongly influences your home life and family relationships. This figure is associated with your family, your ancestors, and your sense of belonging. It also relates to your emotional well-being and your overall state of mind.

If the figure is well-aspected, it indicates that you likely have a happy home life and a close relationship with your family. If the figure is poorly-aspected, it suggests that you may have problems with your family or your emotional health. Either way, the 4th House figure is an important indicator of your relationship with your home and family.

When interpreting a figure in the 4th House, it is important to pay attention to the element and quality of the figure, as well as the planet that rules it. This will give you clues as to how the figure will manifest in your home life and family relationships. For example, a Fire element figure in the 4th House indicates that you are likely passionate and fiery in your relationships with your family. A Water element figure in the 4th House suggests that you are likely compassionate and introspective in your relationships with your family.

House of Creativity

The geomantic figure in the 5th House strongly influences your creativity and self-expression. This figure is associated with your hobbies, creative projects, and love life. It also relates to your sense of fun and your overall state of mind.

If the figure is well-aspected, it indicates that you are likely creative and that you have an active love life. If the figure is poorly-aspected, it suggests that you may have problems with your creative endeavors or your love life. Either way, the 5th House figure is an important indicator of your ability to express yourself creatively and enjoy romantic relationships.

The element and quality of the figure, as well as the planet that rules it, will give you clues as to how the figure will manifest in your creativity and love life. For example, a Fire element figure in the 5th House indicates that you are likely creative and passionate in your hobbies and relationships. A Water element figure in the 5th House suggests that you are likely introspective and compassionate in your hobbies and relationships.

House of Health and Work

The geomantic figure in the 6th House strongly influences your health and work life. This figure is associated with your physical health, daily routine, and job. It also relates to your mental health and your overall state of mind.

If the figure is well-aspected, it indicates that you likely have good physical and mental health. If the figure is poorly-aspected, it suggests that you may have problems with your health or your work life. Either way, the 6th House figure is an important indicator of your ability to maintain a healthy lifestyle and to be productive when it comes to your work.

The element and quality of the figure, as well as the planet that rules it, will give you clues as to how the figure will manifest in your health and work life. For example, a Fire element figure in the 6th House indicates that you are likely passionate and fiery in your approach to work and health. A Water element figure in the 6th House suggests that you are likely introspective and compassionate in your approach to work and health.

House of Balance

The geomantic figure in the 7th House strongly influences your relationships and interactions with others. This figure is associated with your close relationships, your marriage, and your business partnerships. It also relates to your sense of fair play and your overall state of mind.

If the figure is well-aspected, it indicates that you likely have harmonious relationships with others. If the figure is poorly-aspected, it suggests that you may have problems with your relationships or your sense of fair play. The 7th House figure is an important indicator of your ability to interact with others positively.

The element and quality of the figure, as well as the planet that rules it, will give you clues as to how the figure will manifest in your relationships with others. For example, a Fire element figure in the 7th House indicates that you are likely passionate and fiery in your interactions with others. A Water element figure in the 7th House suggests that you are likely introspective and compassionate in your interactions with others.

House of Transformation

The geomantic figure in the 8th House has a strong influence on your transformation and rebirth. This figure is associated with your death, your taxes, and your sex life. It also relates to your ability to let go of the past and move on to new beginnings.

If the figure is well-aspected, it indicates that you likely have a positive transformation in your life. If the figure is poorly-aspected, it suggests that you may have problems with your ability to let go of the past or move on to new beginnings. The 8th House figure is an important indicator of your ability to change and grow.

The element and quality of the figure, as well as the planet that rules it, will give you clues as to how the figure will manifest in your transformation and rebirth. For example, a Fire element figure in the 8th House indicates that you are likely to be passionate and fiery in your approach to change and growth. A Water element figure in the 8th House suggests that you are likely introspective and compassionate in your approach to change and growth.

House of Higher Learning

The geomantic figure in the 9th House strongly influences your higher learning and spiritual knowledge. This figure is associated with your higher education, your philosophy, and your religion. It also relates to your ability to see the big picture and find meaning in life.

If the figure is well-aspected, it indicates that you likely have a positive experience with higher learning and spiritual knowledge. If the figure is poorly-aspected, it suggests that you may have problems with your ability to see the big picture or find meaning in life. The 9th House figure is an important indicator of your ability to learn and grow spiritually.

The element and quality of the figure, as well as the planet that rules it, will give you clues as to how the figure will manifest in your higher learning and spiritual knowledge. For example, a Fire element figure in the 9th House indicates that you are likely passionate and fiery in your approach to higher learning and spirituality. A Water element figure in the 9th House suggests that you are likely introspective and compassionate in your approach to higher learning and spirituality.

House of Career

The geomantic figure in the 10th House has a strong influence on your career and public reputation. This figure is associated with your profession, your status, and your achievements. It also relates to your ability to be successful in the public eye.

If the figure is well-aspected, it indicates that you likely have a positive experience with your career and public reputation. If the figure is poorly-aspected, it suggests that you may have problems with your ability to be successful in the public eye. The 10th House figure is an important indicator of your ability to achieve your goals.

The element and quality of the figure, as well as the planet that rules it, will give you clues as to how the figure will manifest in your career and public reputation. For example, a Fire element figure in the 10th House indicates that you are likely passionate and fiery in your approach to your career and public image. A Water element figure in the 10th House suggests that you are likely introspective and compassionate in your approach to your career and public image.

House of Friendships

The geomantic figure in the 11th House has a strong influence on your friendships and social interactions. This figure is associated with your friends, your allies, and your community. It also relates to your ability to connect with others and form meaningful relationships.

If the figure is well-aspected, it indicates that you likely have positive experiences with friendships and social interactions. If the figure is poorly-aspected, it suggests that you may have problems with your ability to connect with others or form meaningful relationships. The 11th House figure is an important indicator of your ability to build strong social bonds.

The element and quality of the figure, as well as the planet that rules it, will give you clues as to how the figure will manifest in your friendships and social interactions. For example, a Fire element figure in the 11th House indicates that you are likely passionate and fiery in your approach to friendships and socializing. A Water element figure in the 11th House suggests that you are likely introspective and compassionate in your approach to friendships and socializing.

House of the Unconscious

The geomantic figure in the 12th House strongly influences your unconscious mind and your spiritual journey. This figure is associated with your subconscious, your dreams, and your mysticism. It also relates to your ability to connect with the spiritual realm.

If the figure is well-aspected, it indicates that you likely have positive experiences with your unconscious mind and your spiritual journey. If the figure is poorly-aspected, it suggests that you may have problems with your ability to connect with the spiritual realm or access your subconscious mind. The 12th House figure is an important indicator of your ability to connect with the unseen world.

The element and quality of the figure, as well as the planet that rules it, will give you clues as to how the figure will manifest in your unconscious mind and spiritual journey. For example, a Fire element figure in the 12th House indicates that you are likely passionate and fiery in your approach to your unconscious mind and spirituality. A Water element figure in the 12th House suggests that you are likely introspective and compassionate in your approach to your unconscious mind and spirituality.

The astrological chart is the second most commonly used chart by geomancers. It consists of twelve houses, each representing a different area of life. When interpreting an astrological chart, the geomancer will look at the position of the planets in each house, as well as the aspects between the planets.

The geomancer will look at the elements and qualities of the planets, as well as the rulership of each planet. Each planet and house will have a different meaning, which the geomancer will use to interpret the chart. This chapter has explored how to use and interpret the second most common chart used by geomancers, the astrological chart.

Chapter 10: Methods of Interpretation

Each geomantic chart can be interpreted for various reasons, and looking at specific things might help with the interpretation process. This last chapter will provide various interpretative techniques that will help you look at more aspects of a chart and do more accurate readings.

In this chapter, you will learn how to do a daily, weekly, monthly, or yearly chart, how to do a general life reading both for yourself and someone else (or even for a pet), and how to do a reading to find direction in life or the right career, to find a location, to calculate how much time it takes until something happens and so on.

Various Interpretation Techniques

Many techniques can be used for interpretation, but some are more common than others. In this section, we will look at the most common ones.

1. The Four Pillars

The four pillars technique is the most common and basic. It involves looking at the four main pillars of a chart and interpreting them based on their meaning. The first pillar is the self, which represents the querent or the person who is having the reading done. The second pillar represents the people and things around the querent. The third pillar is the past, which represents the events and experiences that have led up to the present situation. The fourth pillar is the future, which represents the potential outcomes of the current situation.

2. The Twelve Houses

This is another common technique that involves looking at the twelve houses of a chart and interpreting them based on their meaning. This technique is often used in conjunction with the four pillars technique. Based on the position of the planets in the twelve houses, an astrologer can interpret the chart in many different ways. To refresh your knowledge about the twelve houses, see Chapter 4.

3. The Ten Planets

The ten planets technique is another common technique that involves looking at the ten planets of a chart and interpreting them based on their meaning. The way this technique is used can vary, but often, the planets are divided into two groups of five. The first group is the inner planets, which represent the personal self, and the second group is the outer planets, which represent the social self. The planets are also often divided into three groups, which represent the mind, body, and spirit.

4. The Node Axis

The node axis technique is a more advanced technique that involves looking at the nodes of the moon and interpreting them based on their meaning. The North Node represents the future, while the South Node represents the past. This technique is often used to look at the karma of a person or to see how someone's past life experiences are affecting their current life. It can also be used to look at the potential outcomes of a current situation.

5. The Fixed Stars

The fixed stars technique is a more advanced technique that involves looking at the fixed stars and interpreting them based on their meaning. The fixed stars can give clues about a person's destiny or the outcome of a current situation. The interpretation of fixed stars is often made in conjunction with the node axis technique.

How to Do a Reading

There are many different ways to do a reading, but there are some basic steps common to all readings. This section will look at some of the most common types of readings and how to do them.

1. Daily/ Weekly/ Monthly/ Yearly Charts

The first step in doing a daily, weekly, monthly, or yearly chart is choosing the type of chart you want to use. There are many different types of charts, but the most common are the ones that use the four pillars or the twelve houses. Once you have chosen a chart, you will need to determine the time frame you want to use. For a daily chart, you will need the time, date, and place of birth. For a weekly chart, you will need the time, date, and place of birth, as well as the current week's planetary positions.

For a monthly chart, in addition to the time, date, and place of birth, you will need the current month's planetary positions. This can be done using an ephemeris or an online calculator. Similarly, for a yearly chart, in addition to the time, date, and place of birth, you will need the current year's planetary positions. The best way to get this information is to use ephemeris.

The next step is to plot the planets on the chart. This can be done by hand or by using an online program. Once the planets are plotted, you will need to interpret the chart. The interpretation of the chart will depend on the type of chart you are using. If you are using a four-pillar chart, you will need to interpret the chart based on the meaning of the houses. If you are using a twelve-house chart, you will need to interpret the chart based on the meaning of the planets in each house.

2. General Life Reading

A general life reading is a reading that can be done at any time and does not require a specific time, date, or place of birth. In a general life reading, you will use the planetary positions of the day you are doing the reading. You will also need to know your rising sign, the sign that was rising on the horizon at the time and place of your birth.

The rising sign will give clues about your personality and your overall approach to life. To do a general life reading, you will first need to choose a chart. The most common chart used for a general life reading is the twelve-house chart. Once you have chosen a chart, you will need to determine your rising sign. This can be done by using an online calculator or an ephemeris.

The interpretation of the chart will depend on the planets in each house and their relationship to the rising sign. The planets will give clues about different areas of your life, such as your career, love life, and family life. The rising sign will give clues about your overall approach to life.

3. Relationship Reading

A relationship reading can be done to examine the dynamics of a current or past relationship. In a relationship reading, you will use the birth data of both partners. You will also need to know the current planetary positions. This can be done by using an ephemeris or an online calculator.

The next step is to choose a chart. The most common chart used for a relationship reading is the composite chart. A composite chart is created by taking the midpoint of each planet between two birth charts. This can be done by hand or by using an online program. Once the composite chart is created, you will need to interpret it.

The interpretation will depend on the planets in each house and their relationship to one another. The planets will give clues about different aspects of the relationship, such as communication, intimacy, and conflict.

4. Career Reading

A career reading is a reading that can be done to examine your current career or to explore potential ones. In a career reading, you will use the planetary positions of the day you are doing the reading. You will also need to know your rising sign, the sign that was rising on the horizon at the time and place of your birth.

The rising sign will give clues about your personality and your overall approach to life. To do a career reading, you will first need to choose a chart. The most common chart used for a career reading is the twelve-house chart. Once you have chosen a chart, you will need to determine your rising sign. This can be done by using an online calculator or by an ephemeris.

The interpretation will depend on the planets in each house and their relationship to the rising sign. The planets will give clues about different areas of your career, such as your work environment, your bosses, and your co-workers. The rising sign will give clues about your overall approach to your career.

5. Reading for Finding a Location

A reading for finding a location can be done to find the ideal place to live or to visit. In reading to find a location, you will use the planetary positions of the day you are doing the reading. You will also need to know your rising sign, the sign that was rising on the horizon at the time and place of your birth.

The rising sign will give clues about your personality and your overall approach to life. To do a reading for finding a location, you will first need to choose a chart. The most common chart used for this is the twelve-house chart. Once you have chosen a chart, you will need to determine your rising sign. This can be done by using an online calculator or an ephemeris.

The interpretation of the chart will depend on the planets in each house and their relationship to the rising sign. The planets will provide clues about different aspects of a location, such as its climate, terrain, and people. The rising sign will give clues about your overall approach to the location.

6. Calculating How Much Time It Takes Until Something Happens

There are a couple of different methods that can be used to calculate how much time it will take until something happens. The first method is to use the planetary hours. To do this, you will need to know the time of day and the planetary positions. This can be done by using an ephemeris or an online calculator. Once you have the time of day and the planetary positions, you will need to calculate the planetary hour for the planet that signifies the event.

The second method is to use the astrological ages. The astrological ages are based on the precession of the equinoxes. To calculate the astrological age, you will need to know the year of your birth and the current year. You will then need to find the planet that is in the same sign as the Sun was in at your time of birth. This planet will be in the same sign for everyone born in your year.

The astrological age will give you a general idea of how long it will take for the event to happen. The planetary hour will give you a more specific time frame.

Tips and Tricks

If you want to read a chart, there are a few things that you should keep in mind.

- Relax and clear your mind before you begin. This will help you be more receptive to the information in the chart.
- Focus on your question. This will help you filter out any irrelevant information to your question.

- Take your time. There is a lot of information in a chart, and it can take some time to process it all.
- Keep an open mind. The interpretation of a chart is not an exact science, and there will always be some room for interpretation.
- Be prepared to read the chart more than once. As you gain experience, you will be able to understand the chart better and see things you missed the first time around.
- Always start with your rising sign. This will give you an idea of your overall approach to the chart.
- Pay attention to the planets in each house and their relationship to the rising sign. The planets will give clues about different areas of your life.
- The aspects between the planets are also important. The aspects will give clues about the relationships between the different areas of your life.
- Pay attention to the Moon. The Moon will give you clues about your emotions and your intuition.
- Remember that a chart is only a tool. It is up to you to interpret it and make decisions about your life.

There are a variety of different ways to interpret a chart. You can use the planets, the houses, the aspects, or the rising sign to get information about different areas of your life. The different charts can be used to get information about specific areas of your life or to find a location. The astrological ages and the planetary hours can be used to calculate how much time it will take until something happens.

Conclusion

As we have seen, the planets play a vital role in geomancy. They are the building blocks of our universe, and their energies shape our lives and experiences. By understanding the planets and their interactions, we can begin to make sense of the chaos of the cosmos and unlock the secrets of our lives.

The elements and zodiac signs are important concepts in geomancy. They provide a framework for understanding the energies of the cosmos and how they interact with one another. By understanding the elements and zodiac signs, we can develop a greater understanding of ourselves and the world around us.

The geomantic houses are another important tool that can be used to understand the different areas of our lives. Geomancy is an incredibly powerful and insightful tool that can be used to enhance our understanding of astrology.

In the first chapter of this guide, we introduced the basics of geomancy, including its history and how it is used to interpret the energies of the cosmos. In the second chapter, we explored the importance of planets in geomancy and how they can be used to understand our own lives and experiences. The third chapter delved into the elements and zodiac signs and how they interact with one another to create the unique energies of each person.

In the fourth chapter, we learned about the geomantic houses and how they can be used to understand the different areas of our lives. The fifth chapter explored the importance of preparing your mind for geomancy.

The sixth chapter discussed how to cast the points to generate a reading. In the seventh chapter, we looked at the different geomantic figures and how they can be interpreted.

The eighth chapter covered the construction of a shield chart, and in the ninth chapter, we generated an astrological chart. Finally, in the tenth chapter, we explored some methods of interpretation that can be used to make sense of your readings.

Geomancy is a powerful tool that can be used to enhance our understanding of the cosmos and our place within it. By delving into the history, concepts, and methods of this ancient practice, we can develop a greater understanding of ourselves, our experiences, and the world around us.

Part 2: Ancient Astrology

The Ultimate Guide to Babylonian, Egyptian, and Hellenistic Astrology and the Zodiac Signs

Introduction

Astrology is an ancient field of study that holds great significance in almost every civilization known to man. Whether we realize it or not, it plays a major role in our life, affecting and even explaining our past, present, and future. Astrology gives us a better understanding of who we are and how people see us. It can help us understand our dreams, aspirations, behaviors, needs, and emotions. Reading into astrology can help us elevate numerous aspects of life. It gives us insight into the type of career we should pursue based on how we approach professional relationships, our level of financial security, our natural talents, etc. Astrology can also help us cultivate healthier and stronger relationships because it grants us a deeper understanding of what we expect to receive from others. Not to mention that it helps us understand the personalities and behaviors of those around us.

Astrology is also widely used as a form of divination. Many rely on planetary movements and placements to predict the future and avoid any potential mishaps. It's not much of a surprise that so many people are fascinated by the movement of celestial bodies, whether they read the daily horoscope section in their favorite magazine for fun or turn to astrology for guidance regarding the numerous aspects of their lives, including financial, career-related, wellness, or relationships.

Centuries ago, the sciences of astronomy and astrology went hand-in-hand, further denoting just how important this method of divination was. The study of astrology was first developed in Mesopotamia, where it eventually made its way into India and then Greece during the Hellenistic period. Islamic regions adopted this study as a Greek tradition, where it was learned in Arabic before being passed on to Europe once more. The Chinese also held astrology in the highest regard, where each newborn child was given a horoscope. Horoscopes were also part of the standard procedure when a person had an important decision to make in life. Many people today still believe that astrology significantly influences our personalities.

By reading this book, you'll learn all about astrology's origins and how numerous ancient cultures and their understanding of the study influenced the astrological system we know today. In the final chapter, you'll find step-by-step instructions on how you can make your own Astrolabe. This book is not only interesting, but it also includes an abundance of indispensable information. It is perfect for beginners and experts alike.

Chapter 1: Introduction to Ancient Astrology

Over the last 200 years, astrology has gained a renewed popularity in the West. While many parts of the world have continued to place great importance on astrology over the centuries, its popularity has diminished since the Enlightenment. However, a combination of interest in spiritualism and New Age philosophy in the 19th century led to astrology's development and evolution to what we know today.

However, there's much more to astrology than simply the modern version we know today - there are also several ancient versions still in practice, and these have their own benefits. Suppose you've ever found yourself curious about ancient astrology. In that case, you're in the right place - this book is the perfect way to learn more about Babylonian, Hellenistic, and Egyptian astrology.

Understanding Modern Astrology

Before exploring ancient astrology, it's important to understand modern astrology in further detail.

When we say "modern astrology," we generally mean modern Western astrology. Chinese, East Asian, and Hindu astrological traditions are significantly different and are often unrecognizable to even the most ardent disciples of modern Western astrology.

This form of astrology is generally considered a form of divination and is most commonly based on a person's natal chart. The natal chart is created based on the exact time of a person's birth and consists of a chart of the sky as it appeared at that exact moment.

In modern Western astrology, the distance between the Sun and the Earth is one of the most important astrological calculations. Modern astrology also emphasizes which of the 12 signs a person is born under. This is determined based on a person's date of birth, and the 12 signs are:

- The Ram (Aries)
- The Bull (Taurus)
- The Twins (Gemini)
- The Crab (Cancer)
- The Lion (Leo)
- The Virgin (Virgo)
- The Scales (Libra)
- The Scorpion (Scorpio)
- The Centaur (Sagittarius)
- The Sea-Goat (Capricorn)
- The Water-Bearer (Aquarius)
- The Fish (Pisces)

Zodiac signs also determine the 12 spatial divisions of a person's natal chart. When analyzed, the movements and positions of the Sun, Moon, and other planetary bodies help astrologers make predictions.

However, it should be noted that the most common form of modern Western astrology is a simpler version of natal chart readings. These take the form of horoscopes, which are concerned only about the zodiac sign under which a person is born. This determination only makes up about 1/12th of a traditional natal chart, which is a significantly more detailed and in-depth analysis of the life and future of a person.

Astrology's popularity among esotericists is this high because it not only influenced them, but also practitioners of Wicca, Hermeticism, and other similar belief systems. Some scholars went as far as to claim that all magicians have at least a rudimentary familiarity with astrology. The practice is as important as tarot divination regarding public perception of Western magical systems.

One of the most important elements of modern astronomy is its ability to change and evolve with new discoveries. As you'll discover in this book, several planets were unknown during the period of the ancient astrologists, and thus these traditions do not use these planetary bodies in the astrological readings. At the same time, it's also essential to remember that this does not mean that further understanding of ancient astrology is not worth it.

The Reasons behind Modern Astrology's Popularity

Understanding the popularity of modern astrology can be challenging, especially for people who do not believe in it. However, there are several reasons behind this phenomenon.

The simplest answer to this question is that astrology promises answers to your questions. By reading your natal chart, you can find a resolution to long-seated questions that may have been hampering your ability to live a happy and fulfilling life.

Additionally, the advent of the internet means that astrology is more accessible than ever. In the past, creating a birth chart for a client (or yourself) would require familiarity with various other subjects, including astronomy and geometry. It is simple to create your own birth chart with many online tools at your disposal so long as you have the time, location, and date of the birth. Thus, if you're interested in working as an astrologist, you only need to know how to analyze a person's natal chart, not how to build it.

Furthermore, astrology services are easy to access. Some apps offer quick, short readings, and you can also find astrologers willing to perform personalized readings easily online. Suppose you cannot find someone who lives near you and can perform an in-person reading. In that case, you can just as easily find a qualified astrologer who operates over Zoom.

One theory holds that another major reason for the resurgence in popularity of astrology and other similar mystical practices is that people feel like they no longer have control over their own lives. People no longer feel more conscious than ever of how circumstances outside their control affect how their life unfolds. Astrology returns some sense of control to people, as they can look at their fate and act accordingly to ensure they either avoid or meet with it.

Astrology essentially offers the possibility for self-determination and self-interpretation, which is also part of the reason it is so popular among marginalized communities. For example, it has found a home among the LGBTQ community, millennials who fear what the future holds for their generation, and those affected by major events such as the COVID-19 pandemic and the Black Lives Matter movement. These events can leave many people feeling out of sorts and questioning their place in a changing world, and astrology answers those questions.

Benefits of Astrology

If you're only dipping your feet into the vast pond that is astrology, you may find yourself wondering what the benefits of this practice are. This is especially true when you're looking at a particular form of astrology like modern astrology. You may even wonder why you should learn about modern astrology before moving on to ancient astrological traditions. Some benefits include:

- A detailed natal chart can provide you with a psychological road map and a compass for the rest of your life, offering you a sense of direction and purpose, especially if you feel lost.
- You are offered a new worldview, allowing you to see the world around you from a new angle. This can help you move past negative emotions, such as pain, fear, and trauma, and move forward on your journey through life.
- A natal chart reading can help you better understand yourself. It helps you think back on the circumstances of your life and understand whether there are actions you should be taking and opportunities you have been avoiding that you should be meeting.
- Astrology can help you understand specific facets of your overall existence. Aside from general natal chart readings, several branches of modern astrology exist. These give you a better understanding of various facets of your life, including how to interact with financial markets, the effects of astrology on medical issues, how to use it to understand your romantic and platonic relationships better, and more.
- Learning how to perform astrological readings will also help you better understand people with different personality types. This

will enable you to work more effectively with the people around you and help you adapt to their strengths and weaknesses. It will make you a better friend, partner, listener, and confidant.

Understanding Ancient Astrology

So far, we've covered modern astrology in great detail. However, there's far more to the history of astrology than simply the version we know today.

Astrology was practiced extensively across a range of ancient civilizations. The type of astrology they practiced often differed from place to place, which is why Chinese astrology is markedly different from Indian astrology, which is, in turn, very different from Western astrology.

However, some astrological traditions were connected - specifically, Babylonian, Egyptian, and Hellenistic astrology. Due to this connective thread, these three types of astrology are collectively known as ancient astrology.

Babylonian Astrology

Babylonian astrology is the oldest known form of organized astrology and dates back to at least the second millennium BC. The oldest detailed texts on Babylonian astrology are a set of 32 tablets that date back to approximately 1875 BC.

The Babylonians used horoscopic astrology, and these horoscopes were created based on observing the seasonal movements of the fixed stars and the known planets (there were five known planets - Jupiter, Venus, Saturn, Mercury, and Mars), the Sun, and the Moon. They believed that the actions of the gods influenced human lives, which took the form of the movement of celestial objects.

Aside from using astrology as a form of future divination, it was also an important part of the practice of astral medicine. This practice involved the creation of different remedies for different days and dates.

Astrology also helped influence the calendar creation for the following year, including when festivals and important religious activities were scheduled.

Egyptian Astrology

Egyptian astrology shares some similarities with Babylonian astrology. In 525 BC, the Persians conquered Egypt. During the 1st century BC, the Dendera zodiac was inscribed as a base relief on a ceiling in the Hathor temple at Dendera. It is one of the best-preserved ancient depictions of the stars and celestial objects visible to the people at the time. Two signs of this zodiac – the Balance and the Scorpion – are the same as in Babylonian and Mesopotamian astrology.

However, the more prominent form of Egyptian astrology was Decanic astrology. This form of astrology uses 36 groups of stars and constellations to divide the 360-degree eclipse into 36 equal parts. This gave way to a split of the day into two 12-hour halves. This would change over the seasons, with night and day becoming longer and shorter in relation to each other. The Egyptians also used it to mark the divisions of their solar calendars.

Following the conquest of Egypt by Alexander the Great in 332 BC, Babylonian astrology was combined with this earlier form of Decanic astrology to form the first type of horoscopic astrology. This form of astrology likely led to the creation of the Dendera zodiac.

The Egyptian zodiac featured 12 zodiac signs, each based on a particular god or goddess.

Hellenistic Astrology

Hellenistic astrology is a form of astrology that was first developed during the late 2nd century or early 1st century BC. The texts on this were written mainly in Greek or Latin, and it was practiced in and around the Mediterranean Basin, especially in Egypt, Greece, and Rome.

This type of astrology is a tradition of horoscopic astrology that combined the Babylonian zodiac with the Egyptian tradition of Decanic astrology and the Greek system of planetary gods, the four elements (earth, air, water, and fire), and the rule of the zodiac signs over certain parts of a horoscope. The originator of this form of astronomy is unknown, but some sources name him the legendary sage Hermes Trismegistus.

This type of astrology was the first of the major Western astrology traditions to focus on an individual's natal chart. It used the ascendent signs and 12 celestial houses that are still in use today. Indeed, Hellenistic astrology remains remarkably similar to modern astrology, despite the many changes and evolutions the latter has undergone.

Ancient Astrology vs. Modern Astrology

Given that, as mentioned above, Hellenistic astrology is remarkably similar to modern astrology, you may wonder if there are truly any differences between the two.

The simple answer is yes, there are.

Perhaps the most prominent difference is the fact that ancient astrologers only made use of five planets (Jupiter, Venus, Saturn, Mercury, and Mars), the Sun, and the Moon in their predictions. These were occasionally also known as the seven planets. Uranus, Neptune, and Pluto, which the naked eye cannot see, had not yet been discovered and would not be for over 1000 years (Uranus was discovered in 1781, Neptune in 1846, and Pluto in 1930). These three planets are used in modern astrology despite being understandably nonexistent in ancient traditions.

Additionally, ancient astrology features several theoretical models, making it more challenging for people to learn. Modern astrology is comparatively easier to learn, especially the basics.

Furthermore, modern astrology is far more focused on the psychology of the individual who is being given a reading. While ancient astrology also featured natal chart readings, these were more aimed at exploring how society saw you, your place in society, and what you could do to change that place if you desired.

Modern astrology subscribes to free will, and you can transcend the tendencies seen in your natal chart through hard work. Ancient astrology, however, has a much more essentialist view of the individual and the world, and readings focus more on helping you understand your place in the world than on helping you transcend the will of fate.

The easiest way to think of this difference between modern and ancient astrology is that, while modern astrology focuses on a person's inner world, ancient astrology places far more importance on the outside world. This is best seen in Babylonian astrology. This form of ancient astrology focused primarily on determining events that were of public importance and affected the general welfare of the population of the state at large. An individual's interests were generally unimportant when making astrological predictions. It would take several centuries and the development of Hellenistic astrology until the individual horoscope truly became popular.

Why You Should Study Ancient Astrology

Given the differences between ancient and modern astrology, you may wonder whether it's worth studying the former. After all, modern astrology offers numerous effective insights into a person's natal chart, and ancient astrology can often seem far more challenging and time-consuming to learn.

However, there are benefits to gaining a better understanding of ancient astrology. For one, ancient astrology is essentially the history of modern astrology, and understanding the evolution from one to the other will give you a better insight into modern astrology.

At the same time, there are changes from ancient to modern astrology that many people feel negatively affect how horoscopes are analyzed. Often, important analytical elements were lost due to politics. For example, some key features of Hellenistic astrology fell out of use not because they were ineffective but because of suspicions that Arabs invented these.

Additionally, ancient astrology is focused on a far more realistic interpretation of an individual's chart. Modern astrology tends to view all charts as equally lucky and believes that everyone has an equal chance of being successful in life. Ancient astrology is more realistic in that it acknowledges that some charts are luckier than others, allowing the astrologer to interpret the chart in question in a way that isn't setting up the client for disappointment.

Modern astrology focuses on the internal self, which means that it can often fall behind when exploring your chart's impact on your material life. However, ancient astrology is cognizant that your material life is important and does not shy away from exploring both the positives and negatives of your natal chart, ensuring you are properly prepared for the journey ahead.

If you're hoping to learn more about ancient astrology, you're in the right place. All you need to do is keep reading. This book will cover all three types of ancient astrology (Babylonian, Egyptian, and Hellenistic) in further detail and give you a better understanding of their similarities and differences compared to modern astrology.

You'll also learn to make your own astrolabe, which you can then use when performing astrological readings. Astrolabes were an essential tool for Hellenistic astrologers, and having one with you when you conduct your readings will help you take your practice to the next level. Finally, there will be a bonus glossary of astrological terms, which will serve as an easy reference you can return to at any time during your journey.

Chapter 2: The Five Wandering Stars and the Two Lights

The ancient Greeks were one of the very few cultures that played a huge role in shaping ancient astrology that paved the road to the modern astrology we know today. In fact, many of the terms used in astrology have Greek origins. For instance, the words "planet" and "star" are always front and center when discussing zodiac signs or anything related to the topic. "Planet" is derived from the ancient Greek word planētēs which means "wanderers," while "star" is derived from the Greek word astēr.

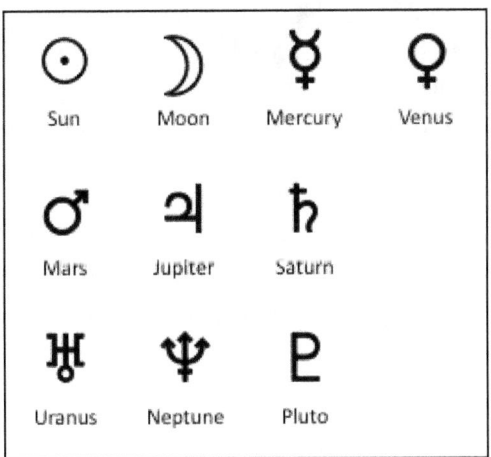

The planet symbols.
Macalves, CC BY-SA 3.0 <https://creativecommons.org/licenses/by-sa/3.0>, via Wikimedia Commons https://commons.wikimedia.org/wiki/File:Planets_symbols.png

By observing the night sky, the ancient Greeks discovered five planets out of the eight ones in the solar system since they were bright and close enough to be seen with the naked eye. This includes Venus, Mercury, Jupiter, Mars, and Saturn—also known as the "wandering stars," or *astēr planētēs*. The ancient Greeks chose the name "wandering stars" because these planets wandered from their path, unlike the "fixed stars" that appear in the same arrangement in the sky every night. The rest of the planets were discovered centuries later after the invention of the telescope.

It wasn't just the ancient Greeks who were fascinated with the "wandering stars." The ancient Babylonians were also known to record the cycles of these five planets because they were curious about their positions in the sky, even assigning meanings to these positions. The people of ancient times did more than just study these heavenly bodies—the moon and the sun were tracked too, and their movements were observed. They were referred to as the two lights or the luminaries, derived from the Late Latin word luminarium, which means light.

The ancient Greeks, Babylonians, Egyptians, Sumerians, Indians, Chinese, and other ancient cultures associated the planets with some of their gods and goddesses. Each of the five wandering stars was named thousands of years ago after either an ancient goddess or god, with each name having a specific meaning and relating to the type of energy each planet gives.

Planets are divided into two categories in astrology: benefic and malefic. Benefic planets usually have a more positive influence on the horoscope and birth chart than malefic planets, which usually have a negative or bad influence. Benefic planets mean pleasant surprises are coming your way, while malefic planets indicate challenging times. That said, the terms malefic and benefic don't have a huge influence in Western astrology as they do in ancient Greek and Vedic astrology. However, familiarizing yourself with the concept will help you better understand astrological transits and your birth chart.

So which planets are benefic? Which planets are malefic? What is the secret behind each planet's name? You'll find the answers to these questions and more in this chapter.

Mercury

Mercury is the first planet in the solar system and the closest one to the Sun. It is a small planet. You may have heard the term "Mercury retrograde" before. That is a phenomenon that occurs when planets spin backward around the Sun. You are probably thinking, can planets orbit in reverse? Well, not exactly. The planets don't move in reverse per se; it is more of an optical illusion that makes them seem like they do. In reality, the Earth is spinning faster as it finishes its orbit around the Sun. Since we are the ones moving faster, it seems that the planets are moving backward when observed from the Earth.

Although all planets retrograde, Mercury's retrograde is the most common and discussed one. This is because the planet retrogrades about three or four times each year, which can negatively affect our lives. Astrologers believe that when planets retrograde, we can feel its impact on ourselves and every aspect of our lives. Since Mercury rules our communication skills, so you may struggle to find the right words for days or weeks. You may even experience arguments and misunderstandings more often during it.

What Deities Are Associated with Mercury?

Mercury was named after the Roman messenger of the gods with the same name, who was also the god of merchants and travelers. Unlike Earth, it only takes Mercury 88 days to rotate around the Sun, making it the fastest solar planet. This makes the name Mercury perfect for this planet since the Roman God Mercury has wings which make him very fast.

The planet is associated with Mercury's counterpart in Greek mythology, Hermes, who was also the messenger of the gods. Mercury is also associated with the ancient Egyptian god Djehuty (or Thoth as referred to by the Greeks), who was also the messenger of the gods and invented writing and languages. The association with the god Djehuty is befitting since Mercury rules over our communication skills and thought processes. The planet is also associated with the Babylonian messenger of the gods Nabu, the god of literature, scribe, and wisdom.

Is Mercury Benefic or Malefic?

Mercury is considered a benefic planet.

What Is Mercury Known As?

Mercury is known as the glistening one because it is one of the brightest objects in the sky.

What Does Mercury Do?

Mercury rules over communication skills, intellect, and memory. It is the lens you see the world through. It serves as a messenger, just like the gods it is associated with and helps you deliver your words and thoughts to others. You can learn a lot about a person by talking and communicating, so Mercury can help a person make a strong first impression. It is through this planet that we establish connections with other people.

What Is the Energy of Mercury Known For?

Mercury represents mental energy and intelligence. It also helps us make declarations and say what is on our minds. Simply put, Mercury's energy helps us communicate our thoughts and feelings.

In Which Sign Is Mercury Exalted?

Virgo.

In Which Sign Is Mercury Depressed?

Pisces.

N.B. *To better understand what it means for a planet to be exalted or depressed, look at the glossary at the end of the book.*

Venus

Venus is two places from the sun. It is one of the brightest heavenly bodies in the night sky. The planet can be seen with the naked eye right before dawn and just before sunset. For this reason, the ancient Egyptians and Greeks mistook Venus for two planets. They referred to one as the morning star and the other as the evening star. It wasn't until the Hellenistic period discovered that it was actually one planet.

What Deities Are Associated with Venus?

Venus was the Roman goddess of beauty and romance or love. Unlike all the other planets named after male deities, Venus is the only planet named after a goddess. In Greek mythology, Venus is associated with Aphrodite, the goddess of love and beauty. Its Egyptian counterpart Isis is the goddess of love, magic, motherhood, and fertility. In Babylonian mythology, the planet is associated with the goddess of sexual love and war, Ishtar.

As one of the brightest and most beautiful planets, it is no wonder it was named after goddesses associated with love and beauty. Venus also has a feminine mystique and features.

Is Venus Benefic or Malefic?

Venus is considered a benefic planet as it positively impacts your interpersonal relationships and supports your interactions with the people in your life.

What Is Venus Known As?

Venus is known as the "morning star" or "evening star," as mentioned above. As the shiniest planet in the sky, Venus is known for its exceptional brightness because the planet's surface reflects most of its sunlight into space. It is also one of the closest planets to Earth, making it easy to see it shining in the sky. Venus is also referred to as Earth's twin since they resemble one another in density and size.

What Does Venus Do?

Venus rules over love, beauty, adoration, pleasure, and luxury. The planet also guides us in approaching love, romance, affection, relationships, and sensual pleasures. Venus is associated with charm, grace, and our love for art. Simply put, whatever makes us happy, is associated with this planet. It is through Venus that you feel attracted to other people and things like a job or a car. Venus also brings harmony and peace to your life.

What Is the Energy of Venus Known For?

Venus's energy impacts aesthetics, creativity, fashion, knowledge, wisdom, and feminine energy.

In Which Sign Is Venus Exalted?

Pisces.

In Which Sign Is Venus Depressed?

Virgo.

Mars

Mars is the fourth planet from the Sun and is considered very close to Earth. Unlike the feminine planet Venus, Mars is associated with masculinity which is where the title of the popular book "Men are from Mars, Women are from Venus" came from.

What Deities Are Associated with Mars?

Mars is named after the Roman god of war, Mars. In Greek mythology, the planet is named after the Greek god of war, Ares, who was Aphrodite's husband. Two moons circle Mars—Deimos, meaning 'dread,' and Phobos, meaning 'fear,' both of whom are sons of Ares, the Roman god. Ares had a chariot called "the chariot of terror" that he often rode with his sons Deimos and Phobos. In ancient Egypt, Mars was called Har Decher, the red one, while the Babylonians called it Nergal, meaning the god of war, death, fire, and destruction.

Ancient cultures associated Mars with war, destruction, and bloodshed due to the planet's red color, which is the same color as blood.

Is Mars Benefic or Malefic?

Mars is a malefic planet. There is no surprise here for a planet associated with war, blood, and death. Mars can interfere with the good things in your life by adding tension and negativity.

What Is Mars Known As?

Mars is known as the red planet. The reason behind the planet's red color is that it contains a lot of rocks that are full of iron. When the rocks and the planet's surface area are exposed to various weather factors, they oxidize and turn into a sort of red color.

What Does Mars Do?

Mars rules over our survival instinct, anger, and aggression. This planet is what drives you into action and adventure and pushes you to get out of bed every morning. Mars is also associated with attraction, but it differs from its more romantic counterpart, Venus. While Venus focuses on establishing deeper and romantic connections, Mars focuses on physical attraction.

What Is the Energy of Mars Known For?

Mars's energy is masculinity and fulfilling sexual desire.

In Which Sign Is Mars Exalted?

Capricorn.

In Which Sign Is Mars Depressed?

Cancer.

Jupiter

Jupiter is the fifth planet from the Sun and the largest planet in the solar system

What Deities Associated with Jupiter?

Jupiter was named after the Roman king of gods Jupiter, a name that fits the largest planet in the solar system. The Greeks named Jupiter Zeus, their king of gods and god of the sky, and he is also one of the most popular gods in modern times. In ancient Egypt, Jupiter was associated with the god of the air Amun, one of the most powerful and primordial Egyptian gods. The Babylonians called Jupiter after their chief god Marduk. As the largest planet in the solar system, Jupiter is associated with the most powerful deities in each culture.

Is Jupiter Benefic or Malefic?

Jupiter is a benefic planet as it brings good fortune and supports all the positive steps you take in your life.

What Is Jupiter Known As?

Jupiter is known as the largest planet in the solar system. It is also known for its stripes and its Giant Red Spot. The planet is covered with thick clouds of different colors, which often resemble stripes, while its Giant Red Spot results from a giant spinning storm.

What Does Jupiter Do?

Jupiter has a powerful impact on zodiac signs due to its massive size. For starters, it helps you better understand yourself and your personality. It is believed Jupiter's impact can affect your financial life and can even make people rich. The planet rules over wisdom, knowledge, and dedication and helps you connect with your spiritual side. Jupiter is the planet of luck and can bring good fortune and prosperity into someone's life. It is also associated with various positive qualities like hope, honor, gratitude, new possibilities, growth, goodwill, mercy, generosity, tolerance, and a sense of humor.

What Is the Energy of Jupiter Known For?

Jupiter's energy is about compassion, optimism, generosity, and hope. This planet can be compared to a guardian angel that guides you using its energy to lead a happier and more fulfilling life.

In Which Sign Is Jupiter Exalted?

Cancer.

In Which Sign Is Jupiter Depressed?

Capricorn.

Saturn

Saturn is second in size to Jupiter and is the sixth planet from the Sun.

What Deities Are Associated with Saturn?

Saturn was named after the Roman god of wealth, agriculture, and time Saturnus who is also the father of Jupiter. The Greeks named this planet after Cronus, who was the youngest of the six Titans, the god of time, and the father of Zeus. The ancient Egyptians called Saturn Geb - the god of the earth - while the Babylonians called Ninurta the god of farming and healing. Saturn is the slowest planet of all the wandering stars; it takes 29 years to orbit the Sun. For this reason, it is believed it was called Saturn and Cronus after the gods of time in both Roman and Greek cultures.

Is Saturn Benefic or Malefic?

Saturn is a malefic planet. Many people are haunted by their past. It can be baggage they must constantly carry to be reminded of how heavy their burden is; this baggage is Saturn's presence in your birth chart.

What Is Saturn Known As?

Saturn is the second-largest planet in the solar system after Jupiter. It is also a unique planet due to the beautiful rings surrounding it. Although other planets have rings like Jupiter, none of them can be compared to Saturn's. Saturn has seven rings made of rocks and ice, and each ring orbits the planet independently.

It is believed that Saturn didn't always have its rings, but millions of years ago, it had a large moon orbiting it. The faster this moon moved, the faster it got close to the planet until it was pulled in two different directions simultaneously. This resulted in a huge explosion, and the remains formed what we know now as the Saturn rings. The remains are still falling on the planet into space to this day. It is believed that they will keep falling until the rings completely disappear.

What Does Saturn Do?

You can think of Saturn as a strict parent that brings discipline, structure, rules, and obligation into your life. It also constantly reminds us of our commitments and responsibilities and how we should set healthy boundaries. It rules over wisdom, expertise, and time. The planet is also associated with karma and wisdom. We can all benefit from learning lessons in life that can help us grow. Saturn helps open your eyes to the areas in your life that need working on so you can finally grow. This planet is all about taking small steps, patience, and persistence due to being one of the slowest planets.

Like a strict parent, Saturn will provide tough love to help you mature and grow into the person you are supposed to be. It can also be a force behind you to help you face your fears. Simply put, Saturn will push you out of your comfort zone so you can change, grow, and become the best version of yourself.

What Is the Energy of Saturn Known For?

Saturn's energy is related to limitations and restrictions. However, you shouldn't see this energy in a negative light. It is meant to help you grow and become wiser and more **experienced.**

In Which Sign Is Saturn Exalted?

Libra.

In Which Sign Is Saturn Depressed?

Aries.

The wandering stars have been a fascinating topic since ancient times and up till this day. We can learn so much about our personality by following these stars and understanding their positions and movements. The ancient Greeks, Egyptians, and Babylonians contributed a lot to astrology by observing the night skies. Observing the stars and their impact on your life can help you learn more about what each planet offers to your sign and how they can impact various areas in your life.

Chapter 3: Babylon: Where Astrology Was Born

Astrology's origins date back several thousand years. Its birthplace is believed to be the city of Babylon, the center of the flourishing southern Mesopotamia around 3500 BC. For Babylonians, the science of astrology was intertwined with religion. Moreover, during this period, astrology was still equated with astronomy, which is a completely different branch of science altogether nowadays. The mixture of eclectic concepts, Babylonian beliefs, theories, and inventions successfully laid the foundations of modern astrology. This chapter discusses what astrology meant to the Babylonians, how they used it in their day-to-day lives, and how their beliefs still affect contemporary practices.

Babylonian Astrology

The Babylonians systematically followed the stars to decipher their fate. However, unlike modern practice – where one's destiny is tied to the different planets and constellations – in Babylon, the future of someone was based on the will of the Mesopotamian deities. According to Babylonian teachings, the creator of the universe was Marduk, the god who later became the patron of the city of Babylon. It is believed that Marduk also set the Moon on its course and dictated all its phases. The rest of the planets and constellations represented other deities of the Mesopotamian pantheon who wandered the skies.

Besides having customs for honoring their deities, Babylonians also developed a tradition tied to the sky's map. They lived their lives by observing everything around them and learning from the teachings of those who lived and discovered fundamental rules before them. Their astronomers observed changes in rivers' water levels and other natural occurrences, followed by historical and economic events. As recorded in clay tablets recovered from the archaeological finds on the territory of ancient Babylon, astronomers at the time had so-called "regular watchings." They conducted these observations on the top of ziggurats, high-rising structures with an open terrace built for this exact purpose. From there, we know that for them, all earthly events were linked to the movements of the sky. They used the constellations to form a calendar for harvest and farming activities. This tradition was adopted by the Greeks and later by Western cultures.

It's important to note that the astrological roles of celestial objects did not take away their roles as deities. Their divine functions still remained, but people learned to understand why they exist and how they impacted life on Earth and thus could prepare for these effects by acting accordingly. Each movement in the sky was seen as a way for the deities to prepare people for events that would take place on Earth. Since Marduk is also a Sun deity, the actions of this god were first tied to Earth. The Babylonians understood that the Sun provides light and heat and enhances soil fertility. Hence, it's indispensable for the survival of plants, animals, and human civilization. Because of this, tracking its movements was essential during the active agricultural stages such as planting, harvesting, hunting, etc. While the Moon was initially seen as a guide during the night, tracking it soon became just as fundamental for the success of the agricultural season. The stars were seen as deities with less significant roles – and by themselves, they rarely left a measurable impression on astronomers. However, when observed as a constellation, the stars revealed many present and future events Babylonians could prepare for. The early records of Babylonian astronomers don't indicate a direct link between constellations and earthly events. However, they noted that these constellations could affect the impact of the other celestial objects. The Babylonians personified the winds, the rise of water levels, and other natural events as gods because they were seen as the actions of deities. And after the observations were made about the constellations, they started to identify stars in the same way. This was, once again, mainly due to the Babylonian astronomers' ability to combine religion, astronomy, and astrology. By applying this complex network of theories, they formed a system that provided a connection between the stars of the universe and the occurrences on Earth.

The basis for both the rustic and the divine roles of the constellation changes can be found in fundamental laws of physics and mathematical calculations used to prove them. Using these, Babylonians made precise predictions about planetary motions, despite the lack of equipment for sighting objects or calculating their movements, just as we have in modern times.

There were, however, some discrepancies between the Babylonian description of planetary systems and what modern science has since uncovered. For example, according to Babylonians, celestial bodies moved in an arc. And because their astronomers didn't understand the complex configuration of the solar system, they believed this arc to be reversible, causing the bodies to move in what's known today as retrograde motion.

After millennia of observations and learning from the variable success of their predictions, they've improved this theory by adding the Moon as another determining factor in the movements of the other celestial bodies. Although they didn't understand lunar movements, they still noted that the variability of activities increased during the new Moon phase. Nevertheless, their observations of the Moon ultimately led to the creation and the following of the lunar month – another tradition widely accepted in modern astrology. After understanding the changes in planetary velocity, they learned to predict known astrological points using the same principle modern science applies to waves. From this, Babylonians deduced that the motions of the other celestial bodies result from the Earth's movement around the Sun. Although this theory has since been disproven, it led to different hypotheses about the meaning of these events. Some of these are still applied in modern times.

Over time, the calculated mappings of the Babylonians led to the evolution of a reliable calendar that could foresee eclipses in the future and determine when they happened in the past. This allowed them to learn about the past's celestial and earthly events. Despite the complexity of the calculations needed for this and the lack of equipment on their part, Babylonians revealed issues that endangered them in the past with high accuracy, allowing future generations to avoid them.

Nowadays, we know that our brain creates images and predictions based on the stimuli generated in our optic nerve as we observe the world around us. The work of the Babylonian astronomers is, in fact, one of the earliest examples of this theory. By combining scientific observations and theoretical understanding, they enormously contributed to their thriving society. Each generation was able to leave this knowledge behind for the next generations, empowering them to achieve more and learn more about the connection between the celestial bodies and the happenings on Earth. This allowed the Babylonian civilization to develop more productive harvest, farming, and trading practices and leave behind a unique scientific legacy. The Babylonian way of observing life inspired philosophers and scientists who lived through the many centuries after their ancient civilization. Not only that, but their traditions tied together religious beliefs and the concepts of astronomy and astrology. And while, in modern times, not all three ideas are used together at all times, you'll still find at least two of them working in tandem. For example, the most accurate astrological predictions are still made by observing the movement of the different planets and constellations – just as it was done in Babylon.

Zodiac Signs

Babylonian astronomers followed and predicted that the Sun's, Moon's, and planets' positions weren't the only celestial movements. While there are no references to astrological houses in the Babylonian cuneiform inscriptions, there is clear evidence that they made observations about zodiac signs. Between 1000 BC and 500 BC, astronomers recorded the positions of the Sun, the Moon, and all the other visible celestial bodies each time they observed on top of a ziggurat.

The descriptions of the 12 zodiac signs in Babylonian astrology are derived from a combination of religious ideas and constellations observed by applying astronomical principles. Although the term "zodiac" was devised later by the Greeks, the Neo-Babylonians named the signs.

Aries is "The Hired Man"
Taurus is "The Stars"
Gemini is "The Twins"
Leo is "The Lion"
Cancer is "The Crab"
Virgo is "The Barley stalk"

Libra is "The Balance"
Pisces is "The Tails"
Sagittarius is "The Pabilsag"
Scorpio is "The Scorpion"
Capricorn is "The Goat-Fish"

The Greeks renamed the constellations as soon as they adopted them. Each zodiac sign corresponds to a constellation through which the Sun and the other planets pass over each month.

With some exceptions, the dependence of the modern astrological nomenclature on its Babylonian ancestor is undeniable - and this is even because when adopted by the Greeks, the zodiac signs only came to be seen as a combination of stars. Both modern astrology and astronomy recognize the importance of this dependence. After all, it provided the foundation for modern scientists to develop theories on the accurate stations of all the celestial bodies. Once again, developing divinatory practices is only one of the purposes of observing constellations. More and more people are discovering the usefulness of following lunar cycles for bettering their life, not to mention getting the most out of the Sun's power throughout the year.

Astrolabes

Apart from the numerous text recordings of the knowledge gathered by their scholars, Babylonians also left behind several inventions that stood as testimony to their scientific advancements. One of these inventions was the *astrolabe*, a seemingly primitive device that revolutionized science soon after its appearance. This device furthered the development of sciences, such as mathematics, physics, astronomy, and astrology. Astrolabes are essentially the almanacs of the celestial bodies. They indicate the position of planets with incredibly sharp accuracy and many other information astrologers need for navigating between and below the stars. Since Babylonians relied on astrology to predict the weather condition, astrolabes were a great help during the agricultural season. In addition to this role, astrolabes were also a reliable navigation tool. Not only do these functions were essential at the time of their invention, but they continue to inspire the makers of modern analog gadgets like mechanical watches with navigation features. Even in modern times, astrolabes can be used to determine your location and the exact time. They can also reveal your horoscope and make decisions about your future.

The original astrolabe was made from papyrus – and it consisted of a central disk (or matter) and a stack of sliding features arranged around the disk. Within the disk is a plate with a two-dimensional projection of the latitudinal lines of the Earth. Over this is a similarly shaped plate called the "rete," which illustrates the locations of celestial bodies. The linear feature above the second plate could be aligned with the time measurements on the central disk. On the back of the disk is a device designed to determine the altitudes of the start. The latter is often used as a starting point – particularly when calculating distance. Initially, Babylonians only used one plate that determined the latitude in one geographical area. As the popularity of astrolabes grew, they realized that travelers often needed to adjust to different latitudes due to the difference in geographical locations they visited on their voyages. Their solution to this problem was to produce astrolabes with latitude plates associated with the world's major cities.

MUL.APIN

Even though it contains a much shorter text than most of their written records, *MUL.APIN* is one of the most crucial astronomy texts left behind by the ancient Babylonians. The document is named after the first line of the text, as it is customary for archeological treatises from the Mesoptamina era. This first line contains the name of the constellation "The Plough," which, nowadays, you can identify by searching around the constellations of Triangulum, Cassiopeia, and Andromeda.

There are a little over 60 copies of MUL.APIN – with the oldest one dating back to around 686 BC and the youngest one dating back to approximately 300 BC. Other archaeological evidence from the same region suggests that most of the data for the oldest copies have been gathered around 1000 BC or before. Although many copies have been found in different geographical locations, there are very few variations in the 400 lines of text the document contains. The lack of discrepancies strongly contributes to the stability and reliability of this astrological compendium. There are, however, slight differences in the complexity of the texts in each list. This indicates that the data for the different lists were compiled over some time. For instance, the first list contains low-complexity texts – but as Babylonian astrologists took more and more time for observation, the complexity of the text slowly started to increase.

In two different tablets, MUL.APIN contains the name, position, and movements of the most influential celestial bodies, culmination dates, shadow measurements, weather patterns, and much more information based on the Babylonian star map. The first tablet can be a valuable tool for those wanting to reconstruct the original map because it incorporates data on the locations of various constellations with the calendar and each other. To reveal the Babylonian star map, you have six different sections at your disposal. These list the major stars and constellations allocated per three different latitudes (33, 23, and 15 stars, respectively), the attributes of the deities linked to them, and heliacal rising dates of many stars as per a 360-day calendar year. The first tablet reveals a list of constellations and stars that set and rise synchronously, the number of days between the rising of those that move asynchronously, and the list of objects that culminate around the same time. In addition, you'll find the Babylonian ancestors of the zodiac signs as part of the constellation group on the Moon's path.

Interestingly enough, the first tablet of the MUL.APIN reveals a year composed of 12 months as the ideal calendar year when Babylonians used calendars of 13 months based on the movements of the Moon and Sun. The difference between the lunisolar year and the ideal calendar year may seem difficult to grasp, but it doesn't necessarily have to be. Supposing that each month has the ideal number of 30 days makes a 12-month calendar much easier to track. In this case, every solstice would fall on the 15th of the fourth and tenth months, while the equinoxes would fall on the first and seventh months.

The second tablet of the MUL.APIN sparked an even greater interest for scientists and historians alike. It provides a comprehensive insight into the ancient wisdom of Babylonian astrology, allowing the readers to make calculations for predicting the movements of the Sun, Moon, and planets. It also provides the unique ability to trace back these events and explore them in the past. It contains the names of all the celestial bodies that travel on the same path as the Moon. From it, you can learn which solstices and equinoxes fall under the full Moon and familiarize yourself with lunar and solar cycles in general. You can see the duration of the nights and days during the major festivities and a mathematical scheme to calculate the rising of the Moon for each month. The tablet also enumerates the stars linked to the four directional winds and the date when the Sun is located in one of the three stellar paths described on the first tablet. There is an approximate date on which each planet is visible – and some recommendations on using all the previously mentioned in the text.

Last but not least, this tablet also reveals a list of astrological omens. Since omens played a fundamental part in the Mesopotamian belief systems, they were said to be messages coming directly from their deities. Babylonians placed heavy emphasis on staying in favor of the gods. They created the omens to engage with their gods and to communicate with them. They used omens during rituals and offerings or as a celestial tie to another planet. Planets are gods' physical and astrological representation, meaning they have a significant part in causing omens to appear. Understanding how omens work and how to decipher them can serve as divination tools even in modern times. This particularly applies if you seek specific information about future astrological events. However, as the information on this list seems incomplete, this may imply the existence of a third tablet - one that has yet to be found. There are two different formats for the omens listed on this tablet. One indicates the occurrence, while the other implies the appearance of omens. The first one suggests that an omen can occur anytime. Whereas the latter means that the omen will appear at a specific time.

Chapter 4: Egyptian Astrology and the Decans

No one can deny the impact ancient Egyptians have on various fields like mathematics, writing, architecture, medicine, and astrology. They weren't just interested or fascinated with astrology. It played a major role in their everyday life as well. They believed their deities appeared to them in various forms, and each of their gods and goddesses was associated with a star or a planet. According to ancient Egyptian mythology, Thoth, the god of the moon, writing, and learning (Hermes in Greek mythology), taught various subjects, including astrology, to his priests and disciples. He also believed that he wrote four books about astrology and carved magical teachings about heavenly bodies on temple walls.

The ancient Egyptians believed that whatever happens in the cosmos can influence each person's life and result in environmental changes. For this reason, temple priests paid a lot of attention to astrology by observing the stars, their movements, and their positions. They designed their temples to help them monitor the stars by incorporating arch ceilings in the temples so they would look like the heavens. For their rituals, the temple priests would only schedule and perform them during planetary activities.

During ancient times, astrology was still relatively new, so there was no such thing as an astrologer. The ancient Egyptians believed astrology was divine, so temple priests were the only ones who acted as astrologers back then. They recorded all the information they gathered from monitoring the stars to understand better how the cosmos can affect someone's personality and mood. The ancient Egyptians were inspired by how the Greeks designated their zodiac signs and decided to do the same by applying it to their gods.

Ancient Egyptians put so much stock in astrology and believed the movements of the stars could help them predict disasters like floods and famine; they even used it to determine the best time to plant their crops. Unlike how people nowadays use astrology, ancient Egyptians took it very seriously. They considered it to be sacred and that it was given to them by the gods. Astrology wasn't just used for predictions; it was used in various areas of their lives as well. For instance, astrology played a huge role in medicine and helped treat people with various diseases.

The ancient Egyptians used a calendar as well. The Gregorian calendar we use now is quite similar to the ancient Egyptian calendar, as they are both considered solar calendars. That said, there are some differences. Both calendars have 365 days a year; however, there are only three seasons a year, with each season consisting of 120 days. You have probably noticed that there are still five days left in the year. The ancient Egyptians added an extra month for these five days, but this month wasn't considered a part of the year. There were also 12 months, like in the Gregorian calendar, named after their main festivals or numbered within each season.

Weeks were also different in the ancient Egyptian calendar; each week was ten days instead of seven, with only three weeks a month. The ten-day week was called "decan," and there were 36 decans a year. The last two days of every decan (week) were like a weekend when royal craftsmen took time off.

Ancient Egyptian Astrology vs. Babylonian Astrology

As mentioned, Babylonians are believed to be the ones who invented astrology, so it makes sense that they heavily influenced the ancient Egyptians. The Babylonian culture influenced ancient Egyptian astrology in various ways. For starters, to calculate Mercury's position in the sky, the ancient Egyptians used Babylonian methods. Around 330 B.C, Egypt was conquered by Alexander the Great, who then created the city of Alexandria, which is still standing today. Alexandria was the birthplace of the Egyptian zodiac signs by integrating Decanic astrology with the Greek

Babylonian astrology.

However, the ancient Egyptians managed to stand out from the Babylonians by creating the "decans," which played a huge role in dividing the day into 24 hours as opposed to the Babylonians, who divided it into 12 hours. Both cultures managed to stand out with original and unique creations. The Babylonians were the ones who created the calendar, while the ancient Egyptians created the "decan" and later applied it to the zodiac.

By dividing the stars into constellations and creating what is now known as zodiac signs, the Babylonians influenced many cultures like the Greeks and ancient Egyptians.

Ancient Egypt and Modern Astrology

Ancient Egyptians have influenced modern astrology because they were one of the first civilizations to divide the year into 365 days and the day into 24 hours. Zodiac signs were different in Egypt as they had no interest in the 12 constellations developed by the Greeks. Instead, they opted for the "decans" and divided the constellation into 36 small groups. This made their zodiac signs quite different from the ones we use nowadays. In the coming chapters, we will discuss the ancient Egyptian zodiac signs in detail.

Decans

We have mentioned "decans" a few times in this chapter, and now you are probably left with one question, what are decans? As you know, zodiac signs are divided into 12 constellations, each including various characteristics for people who share the same signs. However, do all people who share the same sign have the exact same qualities? If you look at the characteristics and traits of your sign, you'll probably find a couple or more that don't apply to you. You may have met people born under your zodiac sign but share nothing in common with you. Decans answer the question of why two people born under the same zodiac sign don't necessarily share the same personality traits, hobbies, likes, dislikes, or habits.

Decans subdivide each zodiac sign without impacting any of the signs' personality traits. It helps shed light on different factors of a sign. Each zodiac sign has three decans dividing it into ten-degree increments to help break down their personality traits. Just like a planet rules each zodiac sign, each decan also has a planetary ruler who acts as a sub-ruler to the zodiac sign. Each sub-ruler planet will provide unique qualities for each decan to help you learn more about yourself. In other words, zodiac signs give more of a general idea while decans narrow down qualities with the help of sub-rulers planets, so they are more specific to people born in the first, second, or last ten days of a sign. However, people born on the first ten days of any sign will usually embody the sign's qualities and personality traits because their sub-ruler planet and the sign's ruler planet are the same.

This doesn't affect the sign you were born into at all. For instance, if you are a Libra, you'll still be a Libra – you will just have a decan to help you better understand your personality.

The decans were created by the ancient Egyptians; this invention made Egyptian astrology stand out from other civilizations. The Greeks were inspired by them and created their own decan; they called it "decanoi," which means *ten days apart.*

To learn about your decan, you should first find your degree. Each person has their own unique degree, and you can find it in your birth chart. However, you can figure your decan out by yourself. Each sign lasts for approximately 30 days, with the first representing the first ten days. The second and third are for the next ten and the ten after, respectively.

Decans should have the same element as the sign they are assigned to. For instance, an air sign should only have air decans, not water, fire, or earth. Decans are also arranged in order, i.e., the first decan is applied to the first ten degrees of a sign, the second to the second ten, and so on. When you understand decans, it will finally make sense why two people born under the same sign have different characteristics; they may even be opposites since each has a different decan.

As mentioned, if you are born in the first ten days, it will be easy to find your decan because your sub-planet ruler is the same as your sign's ruler. However, suppose you are born in the second or third decan. In that case, you can follow the Chaldean Order or the Elemental Triplicities, considered a more modern method.

The Chaldean Order

The Chaldean Order is believed to be the first and oldest method created to help people find their decans. This method only uses the five wandering stars and two lights, the Sun and the Moon. Each zodiac sign is assigned three planets (one for each decan). They are usually arranged based on their Chaldean Order, which is from slowest to fastest, and each planet serves as a first, second, and third decan.

- **Aries:** Mars, Sun, and Venus
- **Taurus:** Mercury, the Moon, and Saturn
- **Gemini:** Jupiter, Mars, and the Sun
- **Cancer:** Venus, Mercury, and the Moon
- **Leo:** Saturn, Jupiter, and Mars
- **Virgo:** Sun, Venus, and Mercury
- **Libra:** The Moon, Saturn, and Jupiter
- **Scorpio:** Mars, Sun, and Venus
- **Sagittarius:** Mercury, the Moon, and Saturn
- **Capricorn:** Jupiter, Mars, and the Sun
- **Aquarius:** Venus, Mercury, and the Moon
- **Pisces:** Saturn, Jupiter, and Mars

The Elemental Triplicities

The Elemental Triplicities is a modern way to help you find out your decan–. It divides zodiac signs into threes based on their elements: air, fire, water, and earth. This method is quite different from the Chaldean Order. As mentioned, the first decan has the same sub-ruler planet as the sign's ruler planet. You can then move on to the second and third decans and the associated element positions. This may sound confusing, but it is much simpler than you think.

To help you better understand how this works, take a look at each sign, its element, and its ruling planet.

Air Signs
- Gemini ruled by Mercury
- Libra ruled by Venus
- Aquarius ruled by Uranus

Fire Signs
- Aries ruled by Mars
- Leo ruled by the sun
- Sagittarius ruled by Jupiter

Water Signs
- Cancer ruled by the moon
- Scorpio ruled by Pluto
- Pisces, ruled by Neptune

Earth Signs
- Taurus ruled by Venus
- Virgo ruled by Mercury
- Capricorn ruled by Saturn

To make things clearer, if you are born under Gemini and want to figure out your decan, the first days of the sign are ruled by Mercury, the sub-ruler. The second 10 days will have Venus as its decan since Libra is the second planet in this triplicity, while the last ten days will have Uranus as the decan since Aquarius is the third sign in the element.

This method is very popular in the West and has been used since the 20th century. However, Indian astrologers have been using it way before then.

Decans have proven to survive the test of time as astrologers and individuals prefer using them to understand their weaknesses, strengths, and potential. You can also learn about your decan to understand the different layers of your personality. If the methods mentioned here seem complicated, especially if you are a beginner, we will also help you find your decan and some of its personality traits.

Find Your Decan

Aries (March 21st to April 19th)

- The first decan falls from March 21st to March 30th. It is an Aries decan and ruled by Mars. People born under the first decan are considered "pure Aries" who embody the sign's characteristics and its ruler planet. They are energetic, passionate, ambitious, competitive, independent, adventurous, and confident people with child-like innocence.

- The second decan is from March 30th to April 9th. It is a Leo decan with the Sun as its sub-ruler. People born under this decan live by their principles and are very noble. They are strong-willed, focused, and stick to their goals and ambitions no matter what.

However, with Leo's ego and the self-righteousness of the Aries, people born under this decan can appear smug.

- The third decan is from April 10 to April 19. This is a Sagittarius decan with Jupiter as its sub-ruler. They are independent, intellectual, open, optimistic, and individuals.

Taurus (20th April to 20th May)

- The first decan is from April 20th to April 29th. This is a Taurus decan ruled by Venus. These individuals love living in luxury and enjoy beautiful things that engage their five senses. They are also stable, determined, and peacemakers.
- The second decan is from April 30th to May 9th. This is a Virgo decan with Mercury as its sub-ruler. These people are incredibly charming and can be mesmerizing with their speech and tone of voice. They are more graceful than people born under the first decan and can be a bit shy.
- The third decan is from May 10th to May 19th. This is a Capricorn decan with Saturn as its sub-ruler. They are steady, loyal, and have a great sense of humor. They are extremely disciplined and may seem serious until you get to know them.

Gemini (21st May to 20th June)

- The first decan is from May 22nd to May 31st. It is a Gemini decan ruled by Mercury. They are curious, intelligent, social, quick-witted, and always up for interesting conversations.
- The second decan is from June 1st to June 10. This is a Libra decan with the Moon as its sub-ruler. They are lovers of beauty, enjoy deep conversations, and are very sensual.
- The third decan is from June 11th to June 21st. This is an Aquarius decan with Uranus as its sub-ruler. They are rebellious, independent, friendly, and sociable.

Cancer (21st June to 22nd July)

- The first decan is from June 22nd to July 1st. This is a Cancer decan ruled by the moon. Individuals under this decan are nurturing, sensitive, compassionate, energetic, and caring but can be very jealous.
- The second decan is from July 2nd to July 12th. This is a Scorpio decan with Pluto as its ruler. They are giving and have great

instincts, making them excel as therapists or detectives.
- The third decan is from July 13th to July 22nd. This is a Pisces decan with Neptune as its sub-ruler. They are extremely sensitive individuals who put others' needs before their own.

Leo (23rd July to 22nd August)
- The first decan is from July 23rd to August 1st. This is a Leo decan, and it is ruled by the Sun. People born under this decan are independent, warm, and energetic but tend to seek others' approval.
- The second decan is from August 2nd to August 11tth. This is a Sagittarius decan with Jupiter as its sub-ruler. They are risk-takers, adventurous, and more fun than a typical Leo.
- The third decan is from August 12th to August 22nd. This is an Aries decan with Mars as its sub-ruler. They are ambitious, honest, optimistic, and kind-hearted but can be extremely stubborn.

Virgo (23rd August to 22nd September)
- The first decan is from August 23rd to September 1st. This is a Virgo decan ruled by Mercury. These individuals are punctual, organized, and detail-oriented.
- The second decan is from September 2nd to September 11th. This is a Capricorn decan with Saturn as its sun-ruler. They are responsible, determined, hard-working, good with money, and ambitious but lack flexibility.
- The third decan is from from September 12th to September 22nd. This is a Taurus decan with Venus as its sub-ruler. They are reserved, steady, and quiet and have an impeccable sense of style.

Libra (23rd September to 22nd October)
- The first decan is from September 23rd to October 2nd. This is a Libra decan ruled by Venus; they are extremely romantic and enjoy the finer things in life.
- The second decan is from October 4th to October 12th. This is an Aquarius decan with Uranus as its sub-ruler. They are inventive and social, and they care about other people.

- The third decan is from October 13th to October 22nd. This is a Gemini decan with Mercury as its sub-ruler. They have great communication skills and are considered social, intuitive, and extremely charming.

Scorpio (23rd October to 21st November)

- The first decan is from October 23rd to November 1st. This is a Scorpio decan ruled by Pluto. These people are passionate, intense, seductive, and calculating.
- The second decan is from November 2nd to November 11th. This is a Pisces decan with Neptune as its sub-ruler. They are mysterious, authentic, and creative with great imagination.
- The third decan is from November 12th to November 21st. This is a Cancer decan with the moon as its sub-ruler. These people are sensitive caretakers, and they rarely compromise.

Sagittarius (22nd November to 21st December)

- The first decan is from November 22nd to December 1st. This is a Sagittarius decan, and it is ruled by Jupiter. They are free-spirited, optimistic, adventurous, and non-conformists.
- The second decan is from December 2nd to December 11th. This is an Aries decan with Mars as its sub-ruler. They are confident, brave, headstrong, and always looking for a new challenge.
- The third decan is from December 12th to December 21st. This is a Leo decan with the Sun as its sun-ruler. These people are charismatic and energetic but can be quite impulsive.

Capricorn (22nd December to 19th January)

- The first decan is from December 2nd to December 31st. This is a Capricorn decan ruled by Saturn. They are ambitious, confident, practical, realistic, and disciplined with a great sense of humor.
- The second decan is from January 1st to January 10th. This is a Taurus decan with Venus as its sub-ruler. They are romantic, sensual, hard-working, and enjoy the finer things in life.
- The third decan is from January 11th to January 19th. This is a Virgo decan with Mercury as its sun-ruler. They are ambitious, organized, and intelligent.

Aquarius (20th January to 18th February)

- The first decan is from January 20th to January 29th. This is an Aquarius decan and ruled by Uranus. They are insightful, reasonable, freethinkers, and non-conformists.
- The second decan is from January 30th to February 8th. This is a Gemini decan with Mercury as its sub-ruler. They are chatty, bright, and intellectuals.
- The third decan is from February 9th to February 18th. This is a Libra decan with Venus as its sub-ruler. They are graceful, sociable, and likable. They are interested in all pleasures life has to offer, especially romance.

Pisces (19th February to 20th March)

- The first decan is from February 19th to February 28th. This is a Pisces decan and ruled by Neptune. These people are intuitive, creative, and the least egotistical people you'll ever meet.
- The second decan is from March 1st to March 10th. This is a Cancer decan ruled by the Moon. They are extremely sensitive, sweet, and loyal.
- The third decan is from March 11th to March 20th. This is a Scorpio decan with Pluto as its sub-ruler. These people are calculating, mysterious, spiritual, and can be prone to jealousy.

As it is obvious from the invention of decans, the ancient Egyptians contributed so much to the world of astrology. The ancient Egyptians also divided the day into 24 hours and the year into 365 days. However, their contributions don't end here. There are also the ancient Egyptian astrological signs which we will discuss in the next chapter.

Chapter 5: The Egyptian Zodiac Signs

We have discussed in the previous chapters how priests served as astrologers by monitoring the star's movements. However, when scientists compared early ancient Egyptian findings and predictions with those of later dynastic periods (when ancient Greece heavily influenced Egypt), they found a huge difference between the two which sparked a heated debate among scientists.

Ancient Egyptian's zodiac signs are a very hot topic among historians as some believe the ancient Egyptians created their own version of a horoscope, while others believe there is nothing to prove they had any interest in zodiac constellations. However, when the Greek civilization dominated ancient Egyptians, evidence of zodiac signs and constellations was discovered later in history.

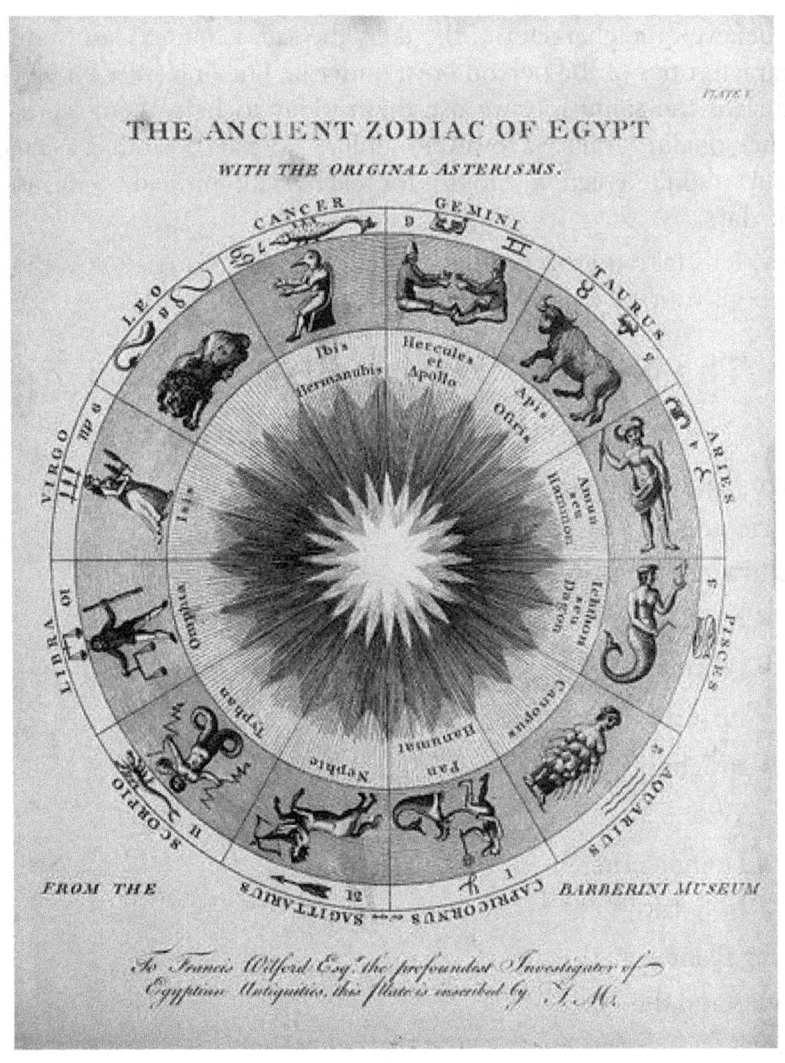

The ancient Egyptian zodiac.
Inigo. Barlow; Thomas Maurice (1754-1824); F Wilford Attribution 4.0 International (CC BY 4.0)
< https://creativecommons.org/licenses/by/4.0/> https://www.lookandlearn.com/history-images/YW024914V/Astronomy-the-twelve-signs-of-the-zodiac

Ancient Egyptians Zodiac Signs

Although Western zodiac signs are very popular, they aren't the only ones out there. Other ancient cultures worldwide have created their own zodiac signs, including the ancient Egyptians. Like the Western zodiac, the Ancient Egyptians also created 12 signs named after one of their deities. However, only one zodiac sign is named after their famous river, the Nile.

It was believed the character of the deity the sign is named after embodies the characteristics of the person born under it. The ancient Egyptians used zodiac signs the same way we use them today to help them learn about their personality traits. However, unlike Western zodiac signs, the Egyptians didn't assign a month for each sign; instead, they assigned specific days.

Now, let's take a look at each of the 12 zodiac signs so you can learn more about yourself from your Egyptian zodiac sign.

The Nile (1-7 January, 19-28 June, 1-7 September, 18-26 November)

Western Sign

Capricorn

Positive and Negative Traits

- Peaceful
- Practical
- Logical
- Insightful
- Wise
- Domineering
- Impulsive

Ruling Planets

Uranus and the Moon

Animal

The Antelope

God

This is the only sign not named after a god. The Nile is an important body of water to Egyptians. They held the river in high regard and considered it the source of life and vital for their survival. Some Egyptians considered it a deity, worshiped it, and prayed to it when they needed something. Today, modern Egyptians still consider the Nile their source of life.

Most Compatible With

Set and Amun-Ra

Personality Traits

People born under this sign are known to be very passionate and peaceful. They hate nothing more than missing an opportunity and would rather act now than regret it later. They dislike conflict and can make others feel calm and at peace whenever they are around them. They are considered very wise individuals, very intelligent, and have strong observation and communication skills. Making friends comes easily to this sign because of their helpful, selfless, and giving personality. They love the finer things in life and hope one day to become wealthy. These people are also practical, cautious, and patient. They are extremely adaptable, which makes them suitable for various professions.

On the other hand, people born under the Nile sign can be impulsive and prone to having emotional outbursts every now and then. They are usually obsessed with details, making them nervous and disturbing their inner peace. They can be a bit moody and go from being quiet and calm to angry and irrational.

Amon-Ra (8-21 January, 1-11 February)

Western Sign

Taurus

Positive and Negative Traits

- Helpful
- Generous
- Powerful
- Successful
- Secretive

Ruling Planets

Saturn and the Sun

Animal

The Ram

God

Amun-Ra is the king of all gods; he created the universe and all of mankind. It is believed that he gave people the ability to create things from nothing.

Most Compatible With

Horus and the Nile

Personality Traits

People born under this sign are optimistic and talented. Leadership comes naturally to them because they are trustworthy. They are highly intuitive; a quality they use to fix any problem they face. They would never say no to anyone asking for help since they are giving people who are happy to lend a helping hand. They are strong leaders, very confident, and remain in control no matter what happens around them. They are very classy; you may even mistake them for royalty. Some of the happiest people you'll ever meet are born under this sign; you'll find them always optimistic with a smile on their faces. They are very lucky individuals who always find success. They are perfect for jobs like motivational speakers, counselors, or life coaches because others find them inspiring and go to them for advice. Great listeners, intelligence, and good decision-makers are all the qualities that make them suitable for leadership positions like managers or CEOs.

On the other hand, they are so focused on their career and helping others that they may neglect their home life. For this reason, they may not be inclined to start a family. Stubborn with a huge ego, there is no going back once they decide. They won't listen to anyone's advice because they can be unyielding.

Mut (22-31 January, 8-22 September)

Western Sign

Scorpio

Positive and Negative Traits

- Hardworking
- Attentive
- Ironic
- Unfriendly
- Cranky

Ruling Planet

The Sun

Animal

Vulture

God

Mut is a female deity. She is the goddess of the sky and is considered the mother of all mankind and the one responsible for protecting them.

Most Compatible With

Thoth and Amun-Ra

Personality Traits

Since Mut is a mother goddess, individuals born under this sign are known to be nurturing and very protective of the people in their lives. However, they also need to feel protected and are always looking for someone who can act as a parent and look out for them. As a result of their nurturing nature, they can also be great parents and role models. They only open up to those closest to them and keep their thoughts and feelings hidden from everyone else. They are very shy by nature, especially in new relationships, but once you get to know them, you'll see how generous and wise they are. Serious and committed in relationships, they can be great partners. They are goal-oriented and know exactly what they want out of life. Focused and determined, they will do whatever it takes to achieve their goals. People are usually attracted to them because they are charming and good listeners.

When it comes to their negative traits, people born under the Mut sign can be too involved in their relationships. Since they are very committed, they usually expect their relationship to last, and when it doesn't, they become very disappointed. They are prone to long episodes of depression and sadness. In relationships, they often seem cold and rarely show their feelings, mostly because they are secretive individuals. They often think that showing affection will make them seem vulnerable or weak. They have explosive tempers and would rather give the silent treatment than talk things out. Mut individuals often criticize others but don't handle criticism very well.

Geb (February 12-29 and August 20-31)

Western Sign

Libra

Positive and Negative Traits

- Fair
- Modest
- Proud
- Sensitive
- Affectionate
- Anxious
- Vain

Ruling Planet

Earth

Animal

Goose

God

Geb is the god of the earth. It is believed that his laughter could cause earthquakes. He plays a huge role in the afterlife as he is one of the gods that weigh the deceased people's hearts to determine their fate.

Most Compatible With

Set and Horus

Personality Traits

Sensitive and kind-hearted, people born under this sign are usually very attentive to other people's feelings. They are highly intuitive and compassionate, making them seem very emotional. They are introverted individuals who always listen to their gut feeling. They can be very empathetic and are deeply affected by anything that happens in the world. As a result, they may avoid watching the news or going on social media to protect themselves from all the negativity in the world. If you ask your Geb friend for a favor, rest assured they will come through for you because they are very reliable individuals. Although they are highly sensitive, they manage to keep their feelings under control and remain composed during any situation. They aren't impulsive; they think before acting. They can be shy at times, but, when necessary, they can also be assertive. They are always there for other people and would never forget it if you lent them a helping hand. Careers like writing, counseling, or teaching are perfect for them. Just like their counterpart Libra, they love the finer things in life and are lovers of beauty.

As a result of their kind nature, people often can take advantage of individuals born under the Geb sign. At times, they can be vain and suffer from huge egos. They don't know how to set healthy boundaries and say no to others because they don't want to hurt anyone's feelings.

Osiris (March 1-10, November 27-December 18)

Western Sign

Aries

Positive and Negative Traits

- Bold
- Energetic
- Domineering
- Bossy
- Indecisive

Ruling Planets

The Sun and Pluto

Animal

Bull

God

Osiris is the god of the dead and the afterlife. He symbolizes fertility, resurrection, and rebirth.

Most Compatible With

Isis and Thoth

Personality Traits

Having a dual personality is an accurate description of this sign. They can either be strong and feisty or vulnerable and indecisive. You'll find that they get excited about the New Year because they love new beginnings and are hopeful about their future. They are innovative and suitable for careers like teaching or sales. People born under this sign can be perfect for leadership positions because they're intelligent and charismatic individuals. For sure, leadership comes easily to them because they are confident and goal-oriented. They are also flexible, can easily cope with change, and are determined individuals who would never let anything stand between them and their dreams. They are direct, energetic, and live in the moment. They are also confident, adventurous, and fiercely independent.

However, they don't like taking orders from other people, even if it is their boss. They may show an aggressive or dominating attitude to anyone above them. Arguing with them can be exhausting because of their huge ego, which can impact their relationships. With the smallest misunderstanding, they may lose their temper and explode. As a result, working with them can be very difficult. They are good leaders but don't know how to follow and can't handle criticism.

Isis (11-31 March, 18-29 October, 19-31 December)

Western Sign

Pisces

Positives and Negatives

- Passionate
- Ambitious
- Dignified
- Straightforward
- Hyperactive
- Demanding

Ruling Planets

Earth, Uranus, and the Moon

Animal

Ram

God

Isis is another female deity. She is the goddess of nature and the protector of children, the poor, and the dead. She is also a mother's guardian as she protects them when they are giving birth.

Most Compatible With

Osiris and Thoth

Personality Traits

You'll never experience any misunderstandings with these individuals by seeing how they are straightforward. They love being in love and always have faith in their relationships. They prefer partners who are carefree and adventurous. They are energetic and have great communication skills and a playful attitude. People are usually attracted to them because of their great sense of humor. They are very protective of the people in their lives and always ready to put a smile on their faces. They are suitable for careers that involve rational thinking and disciplining others like supervisors or leaders.

On the other hand, they can be too demanding, which can strain their relationships. They get bored and restless and often crave change. As a result, they may struggle to focus on their goals and will keep finding new ones and switching between them. This can distract them from achieving anything. Serious is a word they aren't very fond of, and they avoid serious situations like the plague.

Thoth (April 1 – 19, November 8 – 17)

Western Sign

Virgo

Positive and Negative Traits

- Great listeners
- Possess leadership skills
- Compassionate
- Courageous
- Energetic
- Difficult to work with
- Naive

Ruling Planets

Mercury and the Moon

Animal

Baboon

God
Thoth is the god of wisdom and learning. He created writing and is considered the record keeper of everything.

Most Compatible With
Isis and Bastet

Personality Traits
If you are looking for a problem solver, people born under this sign are the ones to look for. They are creative and enjoy sharing the things they have learned. This can make them suitable for a teaching career. They are very organized and have high communication skills. Since the god of writing rules them, they can make great journalists or writers. They are very loyal in romantic relationships and look for stable partners who value family, just like them.

They can be impatient and make impulsive decisions. Naive and too trusting, these individuals only see the good in people, leading them to disappointment when they are wrong. They can sometimes be stubborn and unable to see things from others' points of view.

Horus (April 20-May 7, August 12-19)

Western Sign
Aquarius

Positive and Negative Traits
- Charming
- Wit
- Endurance
- Strong-willed
- Inflexible
- Stubborn

Ruling Planets
The Sun and the Moon

Animal
Snake

God

Horus is one of the most popular ancient Egyptian gods. He is the god of the sky and the protector of the pharaohs. It is believed he was the one that united Upper and Lower Egypt.

Most Compatible With

Geb and Bastet

Personality Traits

Unafraid to take risks, people born under this sign are very courageous. They enjoy trying new things and would never say no to any opportunity. They are very charismatic and optimistic individuals. As a result of their courage, they can excel in any career they choose. Inspiring, motivated, and natural leaders know what they want and aren't afraid to go after it. They are strong-willed, ambitious, and very devoted to their families, putting them first. They are selfless, great listeners, and kind. People born under this sign can help you solve any problem you face. They will excel as psychologists or guidance counselors.

Unyielding, people born under a Horus sign are stubborn and inflexible in their opinions. People may see them as domineering because they enjoy being in charge. They may struggle with their relationships because of their angry outbursts and aggression.

Anubis (May 8-27, June 29-July 13)

Western Sign

Leo

Positive and Negative Qualities

- Sympathetic
- Honest
- Intelligent
- Cunning
- Competitive
- Controlling

Ruling Planet

Mercury

Animal

Jackal

God

Anubis is the god of mummification, death, and the afterlife. He also guards the underworld. He can find those who are lost to life, and he will weigh their hearts to determine if they are worthy of passing on.

Most Compatible With

Isis and Bastet

Personality Traits

Creative, passionate, sensitive, and emotional are some of the qualities people born under Anubis are famous for. They don't prefer to work in teams; they shine when they work alone. They aren't fond of crowds because of their introverted nature. However, when they are around people, they are always confident. They are extremely blunt and aren't afraid to speak their mind. Their curiosity about people, their thoughts, and how their minds work makes them suitable for careers in psychology or teaching. They can also excel in roles that involve helping others, like a doctor or a nurse. Determined, they would never give up until they achieved their goals. Being ruled by Horus, they may have a slight interest in death.

Individuals born under this sign may experience severe mood swings, they can be happy, and suddenly, they are depressed or angry. This can result from their empathetic nature and absorbing other people's emotions. They can be controlling and too competitive and would struggle if someone else was taking the lead. In relationships, they can be possessive.

Seth (May 28-June 18, September 28-October 2)

Western Sign

Gemini

Positive and Negative Traits

- Determined
- Perfectionist
- Persistent
- Impulsive

- Bad-tempered

Ruling Planet

Mars

Animal

Tiger

God

Seth is the god of chaos, earthquakes, and storms. It is believed that he could control the weather. According to an ancient legend, Seth killed his brother Osiris, chopped his body into pieces, and left each body apart in a different place in Egypt. He believed that he did that because he discovered that his wife, Nephtys, had a child with Osiris. This child is the god Anubis.

Most Compatible With

The Nile and Geb

Personality Traits

Adventurous and perfectionist, nothing can stop people born under this sign from going after what they want. They have great leadership skills and can always rise to the challenge. They don't think about the past; they learn from their mistakes and happily move on to better things in their future. Charming, charismatic, and outgoing are some of the qualities that attract people to them. They are social and love being around other people. They don't like sitting still or being idle; they always want to be busy. Their ideal job is teaching.

Bastet individuals are moody and have a very bad temper. They value their freedom and hate rules and restrictions, so they may struggle with being micromanaged or following guidelines. They have a rebellious spirit and find it hard to conform.

Bastet (14-28 July, 23-27 September, 3-17 October)

Western Sign

Cancer

Positive and Negative Traits

- Thoughtful
- Charming

- Anxious
- Clingy
- Possessive

Ruling Planets

The Sun and the Moon

Animal

Cat

God

Bastet is another female deity. She is usually called the cat goddess because she has a cat head and a human body. She is the goddess of homelife and womanhood. A guardian of women, Bastet helps them with their fertility.

Most Compatible With

Horus and Sekhmet

Personality Traits

Nothing is more important for the Bastet people than peace. They are introverts who love peace and quiet and usually avoid crowds, stressful situations, and confrontations. They are extremely intuitive; you may mistake them for psychics. They are charming individuals who live their lives to the fullest. Happiness is their number one goal which is why they surround themselves with things they find pleasing. Fiercely loyal, they are devoted to their loved ones and will always put them first. They are nurturing, sensitive, and emotional and will always protect the people in their lives. The ideal job for them is writing.

In relationships, they can be overprotective, clingy, and possessive. Trust doesn't come easy to them and is usually very secretive. They often remain hung up on past relationships for a long time and struggle to let go and move on.

Sekhmet (July 29-August 11, October 30-November 7)

Western Sign

Sagittarius

Positive and Negative Traits
- Approachable
- Cheerful
- Optimistic
- Clever
- Leadership skills
- Easily offended
- Impatient

Ruling Planet
The Sun

Animal
Lion

God
Sekhmet is the last female deity we have on this list. She is referred to as the Eye of Ra. Sekhmet, the goddess of war and a healer, ensures justice is served as she has the power to decide who is guilty and who is innocent. She has the head of a lion and the body of a woman.

Most Compatible With
Baster and Geb

Personality Traits
Like people born under Osiris, individuals born under Sekhmet have dual personalities. They can be strict and disciplined on one side; on the other, they are flexible and free. They are perfectionists, just, and have strong values. They are suitable for jobs like CEOs or judges. Professional, trustworthy, approachable, disciplined, and graceful are some of the qualities that make people respect them and feel drawn to them. Down to earth and intelligent, they find success in whatever they do. The glass is always half full of Sekhmet people. They have a sunny attitude and charming personalities.

Sekhmet individuals tend to have short tempers. They can be impatient, aggressive, and rude. They can be very focused on materialistic pursuits and can suffer from addictions. In relationships, they can be very possessive. They begin bragging about their accomplishments whenever they feel confident and make others feel inferior.

The Egyptian zodiac signs are very interesting and can help you learn about different aspects of your personality. You should definitely read more about the god of your zodiac sign because all ancient Egyptian goods have interesting legends associated with them.

Chapter 6: Hellenistic Astrology I. The Topoi

Astrology has played a major role in almost every single civilization. However, this field of study's role in the Late-Hellenistic era is noteworthy, particularly because it blends aspects of Greek philosophy and views on an individual's dynamics of life. While horoscopic or natal charts, which divide the sky into regions describing the planetary positions, originated in Babylon, they were essentially developed in Hellenized, Greek-speaking areas. The oldest natal chart dates back to 410 BCE in Babylon. Although the incredible Babylonian advancement can't be understated, Mesopotamians had already used star omens for divination and astral spirituality for years at that point in history.

They used stars to symbolize gods they could pray to and receive favors from. You may have already heard of Anu, Enlil, and Ea, the astrological deities that are represented not only by single stars but also by constellations. The concept of planetary gods can also be found in Hellenistic astrology. Mars or Nergal was believed to be the deity of destruction and plagues, while Venus or Ištar was considered the goddess of love. A limited number of Babylonian records pertain to laconic predictions and planetary placements, making it particularly challenging to draw solid inferences regarding the conceptual basis of early horoscopic practices.

The Hellenistic Era and Modern-Day Astrology

The Hellenistic era is unique, combining numerous philosophies, including Babylonian, Egyptian, Jewish, and Persian spiritual beliefs and ideologies. Astronomy and astrology practices were already spreading in the lands of Babylon before the conquest of Alexander the Great. At that point, Greek thinkers weren't yet concerned with these areas of study. While Greece was responsible for making astrology studies popular, the Babylonian writer, Berossus, and other Babylonian astrologers and priests introduced the Greeks to the science.

Alexandria, Egypt's intellectual hub, is believed to be the home of notable Hellenistic astrology developments. Numerous Hellenistic astrologers credited the pharaoh Nechepso, who was an Egyptian priest, with the earliest and most significant astrological advancements. Hermes, the Greek god of astrology, is believed to be the inventor of astrology. Some developments that trace back to the deity's name still survive, while other authors speak of other works belonging to Nechepso. The Greek Asclepius, Pythagoras, Orpheus, the Egyptian Anubis, the Iranian Zoroaster, and the prophet Abraham are also examples of other figures associated with astrology. Late Hellenistic texts refer to Kidinnu, Sudines, Naburianos, Babylonian astronomers, and astrologers.

The source of Hellenistic astrology, and whether it can be attributed to the Egyptians or the Babylonians, is perhaps the result of Ptolemaic and Seleucid rivalries. The Babylonians and the Egyptians are primarily credited with numerous astrological charts, tables, and techniques. However, modern research suggests that some astrological methods and approaches were inaccurately traced. Egyptian calendars, spiritual practices, and religious beliefs were merged with Babylonian astrological techniques, joined by Pythagorean mathematics, Stoic and Platonist philosophies, and Hermeticism. This created a more complex and intricate astrological system that is close to what we have today.

This chapter illustrates the importance of the diurnal and nocturnal horoscopes for Greek astrologers. Then, you'll understand the word topos (places) used by Greek astrologers in more depth. Here, you'll find out what these places show, how they're calculated, and which astrological houses they're associated with. In this chapter, you'll find the meaning of each place, as well as the similarities and differences they have with their correspondent houses.

Sect: Diurnal and Nocturnal Horoscopes

The concept of "sect" is very popular in classical astrology, where the seven main planets are divided into two groups. The idea behind the sect is to identify a planet's strengths and benefic attributes in one's birth chart. Although this simple act of grouping was incredibly helpful, it was widely abandoned during the medieval age. The only reason why we hear of this practice today is that recent translation works have restored it.

Sect is originally known as *αἵρεσις,* or hairesis, in Greek. This word was used to describe opposing political or religious factions at the time. For instance, two people who belonged to different heretical groups would be known to be members of different hairesis. Astrologers in Greece ascertained that the planets could be split in two—the day and the night (diurnal and nocturnal) daytime.

Saturn, Jupiter, and the sun all belong to the day, while Venus, Mars, and the Moon belong to the night. Mercury can be part of both and move back and forth. At times, it is a morning star, rising before the sun does. At other times, it rises much later.

Just like two political parties can't be in power at the same time, only one astrological sect can dominate at a single time. As you can probably tell, the diurnal sect steps into its power as soon as the sun crosses the horizon, marking the start of daytime. The nocturnal sect is in power when it's nighttime, and the Sun rests below the horizon. People born in the daytime have a daytime chart where the Sun is in power, and those born at night have a nighttime chart.

Suppose you want to know whether the diurnal or the nocturnal sect rules your chart. In that case, you have to determine the location of the Sun in relevance to the horizon at the time of your birth. If the Sun lies in houses 2 through 6, you have a nighttime chart at the bottom of the chart. The Sun lies in houses 12 through 8, indicating a daytime chart. If the Sun is located at either the 1st or 7th house with whole sign houses, you need to check where it is relevant to the ascendant or descendant axis (the horizon).

Why Is This Important?

As we mentioned above, Sect is used to determine the malefic and benefic traits of the planets. The planets in the sect, or power, are more positive than those that aren't. This means that the naturally beneficial planets are even more beneficial, and those with malefic qualities are less malefic. It is believed that those planets have more "dignity," which is why they tend to behave in ways that will benefit you. As you can guess, the benefic planets that are out of power, or sect, manifest less benefic traits, and the malefic ones are even more malefic.

While this is the main way in which sect is used in astrology, the doctrine also serves as an "auspiciousness" scale for each of the planets. You can look up the diagram to better understand this concept.

Each sect contains a luminary body, either the Sun or the Moon, a benefic planet, and a malefic planet. These exclude Mercury. A sect is then used to weigh the plants' auspiciousness, determining which benefic ones will manifest even more benefic qualities and which of the malefic ones will become less malefic. Ultimately, we are left with two methods of determining the effects of the benefic and malefic planets. This depends on which sect is in power (daytime chart or nighttime chart).

The following is how the planets are ranked in each chart:

Daytime Chart
1. Jupiter
2. Venus
3. Saturn
4. Mars

Nighttime Chart
1. Venus
2. Jupiter
3. Mars
4. Saturn

Mars and Saturn are malefic planets. Saturn is less malefic in the daytime chart, and Mars is more malefic. The nighttime chart displays the opposite.

Jupiter and Venus are benefic planets. Jupiter is more benefic in the daytime chart, while Venus manifests more benefic qualities in the nighttime chart.

The Topoi

If you've ever looked at your natal chart or read about your sign's predictions for the coming year, then you probably came across the word "house." Houses are very significant in astrology, which is why you may be surprised to learn that this word ceased to exist in classical Greek astrology. The word *Topos*, which translates to place or position, was used instead. *Oikos*, which was strictly used to refer to zodiacs as signs, was Greek for *house*. This makes sense because the signs were used to describe the signs as houses for the planets. For instance, the oikos of Jupiter are Sagittarius and that of Mars in Aries. There was never a 1st oikos or a 2nd oikos like there are 1st, 2nd, 3rd, and 4th houses. The Middle Ages, however, was when all the confusion occurred. Interpreters were unsure whether the context referred to houses or signs.

That said, Whole-Sign Houses are the oldest house division technique. As with most other concepts, knowledge of this form of house division was also lost during the Middle Ages. Ancient Egyptian Decanic astrology traditions, which allot a specific topic, such as children, illness, or marriage, to a certain portion of the diurnal rotation, probably influenced the creation of the 12 houses.

The Greek word *horoskopos*, which translates to hour-marker, was used to describe the ascendant. The zodiac sign that rose over the eastern horizon was "marked" by the ascendant, becoming the first whole-sign house. Any sign that entered from 0 to 30 degrees was considered the 1st house, the second one entered from 30 to 60 degrees was the second, and so on. There are 12 houses because there are 12 astrological signs. In other words, if a person's ascendant is cancer, then this sign becomes their 1st house, their 2nd house becomes Leo, and their 3rd is Virgo, etc.

The Houses

The planets that appear in our birth chart and their locations are stationary. That said, the planets are always moving, which means they inevitably change houses. Even though each planet revolves around the Sun in its own orbit, our year is 365 days long, meaning that we experience a full solar cycle that includes all the houses each year. You'll undoubtedly experience the energies of all the houses in your life.

1st House – House of Aries and Mars

This house is also known as the house of identity or self. It is representative of your physical appearance, body, behavior, social impression, health, general well-being, and temperament. The planets that occupy this house influence you significantly. For instance, a person with the Moon in the first house is known to be very emotional. Someone with Mercury in that house tends to be talkative. Planets in the 1st house determine the way others perceive you and the energy you give out. When planets make their way into this house, new projects take off, ideas flow in, goals manifest, and perspectives take shape.

2nd House – House of Taurus and Venus

This house is alternatively known as the house of money, values, or possessions. As you can tell, it corresponds to a person's finances, stability, material belongings, assets, resourcefulness, and progress. Many people don't realize that this house is also relevant to our emotions. The sense of security of a planet in the second house is determined by its material possessions. The planets that transition into this house are related to changes in a person's resources and sense of security. One can refer to this house to learn how they can become self-sufficient while adhering to their personal values.

3rd House – House of Gemini and Mercury

The 3rd house is the house of communication, education, local community, family, transportation, and short travels. It is how you share your perspectives and beliefs with others. Planets in this house encourage you to express yourself and are there for guidance on how you can enhance your relationships with those around you. When planets move into this house, new information about close friends or family may come to light.

4th House – House of Cancer and the Moon

This is the house of family, home, ancestors, and the unconscious. This planet reflects the environment in which you grew up and your experiences. This house is also associated with a person's relationship with their material figure and their general views on the idea of building a home. Planets in this house usually urge us to invest in safe spaces where we can seek protection.

5th House – House of Leo and the Sun

This is the house and creativity and pleasure. It is the hub of romance, playfulness, self-expression, and children. This house relates to your natural means of artistic expression. When planets move into the 5th house, you may experience a period of a confidence boost. This house represents anything and everything that makes you feel good.

6th House – House of Virgo and Mercury

This is the house of routine, health, wellness, and fulfillment. The house's planet determines your spending habits, life choices, and work-life balance. The house of health urges you to pay attention to your mental and physical wellness. The planets here are typically motivated by structure and organization. When planets shift into the 6th house, you may feel compelled to manage your schedule and create habits.

7th House – House of Libra and Venus

This house is that of partnership, relationships, style, and tenor. The planets in this house are concerned with all major relationships in your life, whether they're romantic, professional, or social. When planets transition into this house, you may find deals and contracts falling into place. Things may just become official!

8th House – House of Scorpio and Pluto

This is the house of regeneration, transformation, death, and sex. This house is associated with our animalistic instincts and anything that may be destructive. Birth planets in this house are usually drawn to intense relationships and occult topics. Transitionary movement into this house is associated with understanding the ins and outs of any situation. This also serves to remind us of life's challenges.

9th House – House of Sagittarius and Jupiter

This 9th house is associated with philosophy, higher education, travel, knowledge, and exploration. The planets that reside here determine how we grow our experience and integrate all our knowledge into the different aspects of life. This is a reflection of our journeys and aspirations. A movement in the 9th house involves exploring new topics, adopting different outlooks, or moving to new places.

10th House – House of Capricorn and Saturn

The 10th house is that of social status, popularity, public image, and personal authority. It determines how you initiate changes in your life and the level of determination when it comes to your goals. Career changes and revelations regarding one's ambitions typically accompany a planet's transition into the 10th house.

11th House – House of Aquarius and Uranus

This is the house of friendships and networks, and it aims to remind us of the importance of not just hard work but with whom to share the joy of our successes. Based on your aspirations and visions, the planets in this house determine the types of connections you formulate in your lifetime.

12th House – House of Pisces and Neptune

The house of the unconscious is associated with the hidden and unseen, including secrets, feelings, and even dreams. Karmic relationships are attracted into one's life when planets move into the 12th house.

Showing how numerous cultures can exist together seamlessly, the Hellenistic school of thought served as a promising foundation for the Mesopotamian astrology system. Egyptian beliefs and calendars, Babylonian techniques, and Greek philosophies were combined to create a more complex and intricate astrological system, which is very similar to the one we know today.

Chapter 7: Hellenistic Astrology II. The Zoidia

As you already know, each of the seven planets we're familiar with can be seen moving around the sky in their rightful paths. They come across numerous constellations and stars as they orbit. Make it your life's mission to observe this process, and you will see that the planets strictly wander along narrow paths in the sky - but also move along *specific constellations* - something that ancient astrologers took note of centuries ago. Thanks to them, we now know that planetary paths are ecliptic. The ecliptic can be seen as the shape of a circle that goes all around the Earth.

The Mesopotamians had already started building on this by the 5th century BCE! They divided the ecliptic circle into 12 different segments (30 degrees each). These equal segments were named the "zodiac," a word that comes from the Greek term *"zoidion."*

Even though the word "zodiac" is still relatively popular today, translating the original term "zoidion" is rather tricky because the Greek word has two very different meanings. *Zoidia,* which is the plural of *zoidion,* is derived from the word *"zoion,"* which essentially means "living being" or "animal." However, in other contexts, the word *zoion* was used to describe figures and images. It is suggested that the reason the zodiac was given this particular name can be traced back to the ancient correspondences of the signs. The duality of the word zoidia can be expressed in the fact that the zodiac signs were believed to represent images of the Ram, the Crab, the Bull, The Lion, etc.

Not only that, but this theory can be further expanded upon by exploring grammatical equivocations. The word *zion* may be a locative case suffix. In that case, a zodiac sign would be a place where something else, such as an image or a living being, is located. Another grammatical interpretation, however, may be that the word *zoidion* is a diminutive of *zoion*. This would mean that the picture or the living being would be smaller.

What Would Be a Suitable English Term?

These linguistic ambiguities make it impossible to find an equivalent English term. No similar word in the English dictionary has all these underlying themes and dual meanings. The word zoidion was used for years until a relatively suitable translation was found. At one point, the motion to use the word "signs" to refer to the zoidia was declined. When we trace the English word "signs" back to its Latin origins (signum), we'll find that it was originally meant to refer to images or pictures. However, today, the word is used to denote a broader range of connotations that its initial meaning is no longer as accurate as it used to be. Later, it was decided that using the word "image" to refer to the zodion was the most reasonable option. The concept behind it is that you can use this translation as a base when referring to the "image of the Lion," "image of the Ram," "image of the Bull," etc.

The idea of using the word "image" is practical because you can refer to the zoidia in an abstract sense. In most cases, when dealing with astronomy and astrology, there are many concepts, especially ones that we can understand, that we can perceive with our minds even when we don't necessarily see them with our eyes. The way we comprehend particular *zoidia* is guided by real visual images of the constellations. However, ancient astrologers like Ptolemy did not rely on real-time images of the sky and constellations. This is particularly the case with astrologers who use the tropical or moving zodiac. Instead, they relied on the abstract division and segments of the ecliptic, which we mentioned above. These divisions were believed to be correspondents with specific qualities.

If you delve deep into ancient astrology, you'll find that many texts use the word "twelfth-parts," or *dodekatemoria*, to refer to the zodiac signs. This way, astrologers represented each sign as an abstract segment of the ecliptic. Since each segment or division was believed to be associated with specific qualities, astrologers thought that the divisions were able to give signals, omens, or even prophecies for certain events. This may explain why our modern understanding of the word "sign" no longer denotes an image or a picture but extends to refer to symbols, signals, and indications.

You probably think that we've gone off on a tangent here. What do these linguistic obscurities have to do with astrology and *zoidia*? Well, the evolution of the word "sign" is very similar to how this entire concept is applied in ancient Greco-Roman astrology. These mysteries, and paradoxes, even, have paved the way for an entirely novel understanding of the concept in modern-day astrological practices.

In the 1st century BCE, Varro, a Roman polymath, explained that signs and constellations refer to the same things. Constellations and signs are synonymous because constellations signify something. For instance, Libra is associated with or rather signifies the equinox. For simplicity, the term "signs" (of the zodiac) can be appropriately used for *zoidia*.

Now that you know where the term "zodiac signs" came from and what the zoidia essentially is, we'll delve deep into the origin of the zodiac signs. Here, you'll learn how ancient Greek astrologers used them and how they're different from the ones we use today.

Qualities of the Zoidia

The foundation of the zodiac is primarily built on Mesopotamian tradition. That said, the qualities that later astrologers started assigning to each sign originated in the Hellenistic tradition. According to Hellenistic astrology, one of the most significant roles that the zodiac signs take on is that they influence the way that the implications of the planet appear in the chart. The signs of the zodiac can do so through the following main qualities:

- Having rulership over the planet
- Their gender (this is something that we no longer rely on in modern astrology)
- Triplicity (this has evolved into elements in modern-day astrology)
- Quadruplicity

Numerous other diversified qualities rely on how the constellations look. However, in most cases, these are ancillary qualities to account for and are often used within the framework of certain techniques.

Unlike modern astrology, the concept of systematic borrowing wasn't popular in Hellenistic astrology. This means that the implications of the zodiac signs and those of the twelve houses we discussed in the previous chapters weren't interchangeable; ancient astrologers didn't believe Aries to be synonymous with the 1st house or Leo to be equivalent to the 5th house. The idea of borrowing from a house's implications to obtain those of a certain sign wasn't there.

The Names of the Signs

As you already know, each of the twelve signs has a unique name. The name of each sign comes from its constellation. The zodiac is decorated with 12 bright images of the Ram, followed by the Bull, and then the Twins. The Crab, the Lion, and the Maiden come next. The Claws, which was later renamed the Scales, lies next to the Maiden, and beside it comes the Scorpion. The Archer, the Goat-Horned One, the Water-Bearer, and the Fishes are the last in the zodiac.

While it would make more sense to give the name "The Claws" to a sign like Cancer or Scorpio, for instance, you may be surprised to learn that this was the ancient name of Libra. This is because it was believed to represent a portion of the claws of the constellation next to it (the Scorpion). However, when ancient astrologers started differentiating between both zodiac signs, they renamed Libra "the Scales." If you happen to stumble across an ancient Hellenistic astrology text, you'll find that the term "the Claws" refers to Libra. It was also used in a poetic context.

The following are the Greek names for each of the zodiac signs, along with their meanings:

1. **Aries**: Krios (The Ram)
2. **Taurus:** Tauros (The Bull)
3. **Gemini:** Didumoi (The Twins)
4. **Cancer:** Karkinos (The Crab)
5. **Leo:** Leon (The Lion)
6. **Virgo:** Parthenos (The Maiden)
7. **Libra:** Zugos (The Scales)
8. **Scorpio:** Skorpios (The Scorpion)
9. **Sagittarius:** Toxotes (The Archer)

10. Capricorn: Aigokeros (The Goat-Horned One)

11. Aquarius: Hudrochoos (The Water-Pourer)

12. Pisces: Ichthues (The Fishes)

As you can tell, the English terms for the signs don't look remotely similar to the Greek words (except for Taurus, Leo, and Scorpio) because, to a great extent, the English terms come from the Latin translations of the original Greek words. For instance, the word ram is Aries in Latin, "bull" is Taurus, etc. You will commonly find Greek writings translated literally. This means that upon reading translated astrological text, you may find the zodiac signs referred to as "the Maiden," "the Scales," "the Bull," and so on.

How Ancient Greek Astrologers Used the Zodiac

Ancient Greek astrologers applied their understanding of the zodiac signs to numerous aspects of our being and life in general. While many of these concepts are still applied today or serve as a foundation for modern-day studies, others have been rejected.

Gender Identification

Ancient Greek astrologers believed that the zodiac signs could be split into two groups based on gender: masculine and feminine. Starting at the first sign, which is Aries, the odd ones were believed to be masculine, and the even ones, which begin at Taurus, were thought to be feminine.

Every well-known Hellenistic astrologer accepted this practice. This doctrine was popular to the point where Sextus Empiricus assumed that the Pythagorean practice of naming the odd numbers "male" and the even numbers "female" was influenced by the astrologers of the time. While the association is correct, the Pythagorean theory of the numerology of gender is likely older than the gender assignment of the zodiac signs.

Either way, this Hellenistic astrological tradition was often used to identify or predict genders. According to Sextus, it was believed that the masculine and feminine signs could influence the birth of either males or females. Valens also mentioned that the zodiac sign's gender, which includes planetary indicators for siblings, can help determine the gender of the person's siblings. For instance, if Jupiter, the Sun, and Mercury reside in a masculine sign, brothers are granted. He also suggested that the gender of the signs can be used to determine which of the person's parents will die first. Firmicus also wrote about the birth of twins, where the gender of the signs can be used to determine the sex of the babies.

The assignment of gender to the zodiac signs wasn't only used for gender identification purposes. It was also used as a descriptive aspect in numerous sources. For example, feminine signs were believed to be passive, and masculine signs were perceived as more active. While the former was conceptualized as subordinate, adjectives like "commanding" and "authoritative" were associated with the latter. As you can tell, these correspondences mainly denote gender norms and roles. This doctrine also determined where a person lies in the gender spectrum and whether the native tends to transgress traditional expectations and gender norms.

In modern-day astrology, we no longer use the zodiac signs to predict the gender of the native or where they stand on the gender spectrum. This is perhaps why the concept of masculine and feminine zodiac signs has declined in popularity.

Body Part Assignment

Zodiacal Melothesia, the practice of assigning body parts to each sign, was another common practice among ancient Greek Astrologers. This arrangement is still popular today. The underlying belief behind this practice is that there is a system of sympathetic connections between the human body's microcosm, which reflects the macrocosm of the alignment of the universe during the time of birth.

All systems of body part assignments begin at the top of the human body, where Aries is assigned to the head. The system then continues labeling the other body parts in order of the signs, all the way down to the feet assigned to Pisces (the last zodiac sign). Numerous illustrations of this doctrine were drawn up, which is why it became known as Homo Signorum, or Man of Signs. The assignment structure is more or less the same. However, you may find some discrepancies in the torso area.

The following is the standard assignment of body parts to the signs:

1. **Aries** - The head
2. **Taurus** - The neck
3. **Gemini** - The shoulders, arms, and hands
4. **Cancer** - The chest
5. **Leo** - The ribs, sides, and heart
6. **Virgo** - The belly and abdomen

7. **Libra** - The hips and buttocks
8. **Scorpio** - The genitalia
9. **Sagittarius** - The thighs
10. **Capricorn** - The knees
11. **Aquarius** - The lower legs
12. **Pisces** - The feet

Ancient astrologers used this system to determine the body parts that might be susceptible to injuries and illnesses. Dorotheus suggests that a mathematical technique used to determine a Lot of Injuries, which is a point derived from Saturn and Mars, can be used to predict injury. The native would experience an ailment in the body part corresponding to the sign on which this point falls in the natal chart. This doctrine was further applied in astrological medicine, where practitioners used this concept to determine potential treatments.

General Predictions

This practice is no longer used in modern astrology because it lacks logic and rationale. Ancient astrologers used the zodiac signs to make general predictions, which were often based on irregular patterns or considerations. Ancient interpreters sometimes used certain techniques and general contexts to make predictions. For instance, some signs were considered fertile, while others were considered barren. Astrologers used this concept to determine whether a native would experience difficulties with reproduction. It's important to note that these qualities and characteristics were not standardized, meaning that not all Hellenistic astrologers used the same guidelines and techniques to make their predictions. This is why the qualities were often reported with slight discrepancies.

This level of variability makes it impossible to fully or accurately disclose what the different signs meant in terms of fate or the future. However, the following is a general overview of the qualities and characteristics commonly associated with each sign:

- **Enigmatical**: Sagittarius and Capricorn.
- **Incomplete**: Taurus, Virgo, Sagittarius, and Capricorn
- **Four-footed**: Aries, Taurus, Leo, and Sagittarius.
- **Human in Form**: Gemini, Virgo, Libra, Sagittarius, and Aquarius.

- **Prolific** (abundance in terms of off-spring): Cancer, Scorpio, and Pisces.
- **Barren** (sterile): Gemini, Virgo, Sagittarius, and Capricorn.
- **Royal or king-like**: Aries, Leo, and Sagittarius.

Qualities like mute, vocal, and outrageous were also used to determine the nature of the signs. The constellations and their associated images influenced these characteristics and other rationales or beliefs.

The Ancient Greek *Zoidia* and the associated doctrines and beliefs have largely contributed to our understanding of astrology. Not only did they shape modern-day practices, but they also provided a sturdy basis for additional research. While today's practitioners reject some ancient concepts, others are still widely practiced and accepted.

Chapter 8: The Thema Mundi and Hellenistic Charts

In this chapter, we will go over the concept of "Thema Mundi," analyze its origins and explain why it is vital in Hellenistic astrology. The second part highlights the differences between Hellenistic charts and modern astrological ones. We will also explain how you can transform a modern birth chart into a Hellenistic one.

What Is "Thema Mundi?"

Astrology involves the study of celestial objects and their movements. It is mainly used to predict things that will happen in different people's lives based on the position of the Moon, Sun, planets, and stars. Astrology started due to human beings' attempts to record, measure, and predict seasonal fluctuations mainly caused by positional changes of cosmic objects.

The "Thema Mundi" is known as the birth chart of the world since it was an ancient method used to understand the fundamental principles in astrology. The chart below illustrates the Thema Mundi, which marked the origin of the traditional zodiac sign system.

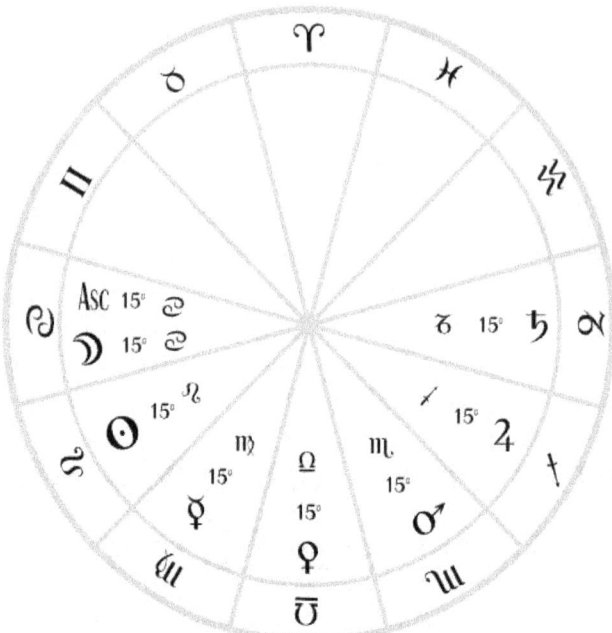

Thema Mundi.
I, Meredith Garstin, CC BY-SA 3.0 <http://creativecommons.org/licenses/by-sa/3.0/>, via Wikimedia Commons https://upload.wikimedia.org/wikipedia/commons/7/74/Thema_Mundi.svg

The signs of the horoscope marked the birth of the world that later came to be known as the Thema Mundi. It was used as a conceptual device or teaching tool in Hellenistic astrology. The system offered a rationale for the sign rulership and specific significations of the signs commonly used.

There were some variations surrounding the Thema Mundi, but all versions have Cancer as the Ascendant. The rest of the other visible planets fan out following a zodiacal order based on factors like speed and distance from the Sun.

According to the traditional rulerships based on the Thema Mundi, the Moon Rules Cancer, whereas Leo is ruled by the Sun. The Thema Mundi refers to "theme," and it also means chart. It was used as a horoscope in Hellenistic astrology that showed the positions of the only visible celestial bodies, including the Moon and Sun, before the invention of the telescope. The Thema Mundi reflects the logic behind aspects like exaltations, sign rulerships, and different meanings of other things.

There was some form of confusion during the late Middle Ages when the horoscope was confused with the Thema Mundi. The Hellenistic chart moves away from believing signs and houses are directly correlated. Modern astrology believes that the first sign of Aries is correlated to the first house. However, Cancer is the ascendant in the Thema Mundi, which significantly differs from modern astrology.

Why Is Thema Mundi Important in Hellenistic Astrology?

The Thema Mundi is believed to show the ideal position of the luminaries and the planets. If you are unfamiliar with the theme and want to learn astrology, you can use the world chart. Since time immemorial, it has been used as a teaching device for astrologers. The symbolic chart of planets shows their positions at the beginning of humankind's existence.

The chart was first used in teaching astrology in the Hellenistic times, as well as traditional sources from Arabic, Greek, and Persian origins used to represent the Birth-chart. It was used as a model for the evolving theories that developed over the centuries.

Another reason why the Thema Mundi is important is that it provides details about the meanings of the seven original planets that appear on the chart. It also discusses the role of these planets in the astrology chart and in general times of life. The Thema Mundi highlights different life processes, including the four qualities and the roots, and finishes the journey with the twelve zodiac signs and houses. The chart also helps practitioners in the field of astrology gain a deeper understanding of its origins.

The Thema Mundi chart provides the positions of the two luminaries, including the Moon and Sun, and the positions of the other planets. It demonstrates the logic behind planetary exaltations and the rulership signs to give you insight into the placement of different bodies during the time of creation. The chart does not correlate with any astronomical event since Mercury and Venus are located very far from the Sun.

It is believed that Thema Mundi came into existence around 322B.C, and it has played a key role in Hellenistic astrology. The theme is still relevant today since it is ideal for novices in astrology looking for ways to evaluate different circumstances. You can also use it to plan for future events, especially if you need guidance. Most astrologers who operated during the early modern civilizations were primarily concerned with fate than individual ambitions. Therefore, not every component of the chart in traditional astrology matters to you. However, reading Hellenistic astrology can go a long way in helping you work out your circumstances, resolve past events, and prepare for the things likely to come in the future.

You can significantly benefit from Hellenistic astrology since it comprises three major subdivisions. The first one is universal astrology, and it is used to predict specific events that are likely to affect many people, like natural disasters or weather-related incidents like tsunamis or floods. It can also be used to predict man-made crises like wars or genocide.

Natal astrology is the second subdivision, and it involves using an individual date and time of birth to create a birth chart. It determines your personality and the paths you are likely to take in life. Katarchic astrology helps individuals pick the best time to perform different activities according to their charts. It can also help you pick the appropriate date for special occasions like weddings.

Different aspects of Hellenistic astrology are relevant today and used in various branches of astrology. However, Hellenistic astrology is set aside from other types by the concept of houses which is still practiced today. Birth charts are used today to determine someone's horoscope and path. Hellenistic astrology also led to the development of the concept of Lots consisting of more than 12. A Lot of Fortune is probably the most important.

What Is the Main Difference between Hellenistic Charts and Modern Astrological Ones?

The main roots of Hellenistic astrology date back to the 18th Century BC Babylon. The Babylon records of the celestial objects are the oldest documents followed in the Western world regarding astrological studies. During the 4th Century, a Hellenistic Greek astrological system was born, which can be traced to the Greek mathematician Ptolemy in the 2nd century AD. The Hellenistic chart was developed, and it includes seven planets, whereas the modern astrological charts have 12 planets, 12 signs of the zodiac, and 12 houses.

Hellenistic charts are a system used to predict events likely to occur in the life of someone, a group of people, or a state. The predictions are obtained through calculations based on movements as well as positions of celestial bodies in the face of cosmic objects that are permanently fixed. The main planets are Mars, Venus, Jupiter, Saturn, Mercury, the sun, and the moon. Planets like Neptune, Pluto, and Uranus were only added to the natal chart following the advent of the telescope. These three planets were excluded from the Hellenistic chart since they were believed to be too far away and could not influence worldly events.

Hellenistic astrology focuses on the outer world and precise predictions of various concrete events, whereas modern astrology focuses on the inner world. Modern astrology is based on natal astrology, which involves using a client's birth chart to help provide psychological counseling. The tropical zodiac is used in modern astrology to focus on future events that may happen in the life of individuals. According to this concept, the Sun greatly influences the events that occur on Earth since it is at the center of the solar system. The relationship between the Sun and the Earth forms the basis of modern astrology.

In modern astrology, all the calculations are determined by the subject's date of birth. This kind of astrology is horoscopic, and the sky is divided to create 88 constellations along the sun's path, which are used for calculations. In a modern chart, 12 signs are used to calculate the position of the Sun when the individual involved was born. It also involved 12 planets and 12 houses that are believed to correlate.

Modern chart points represent different layers of the self, which can be explained using different interpretations like the houses and the planets. On the other hand, Hellenistic chart points show circumstances and people beyond your control. The chart focuses on the bigger picture.

Another notable aspect of modern charts is that they are readily available on the internet and in books. They are easy to understand compared to the complex Hellenistic charts. To understand a Hellenistic chart, you may need to consult an experienced astrologer.

How to Transform a Modern Birth Chart into a Hellenistic One?

Astrology has been used for thousands of years to record or tell time. The Bible and the Quran refer to specific lunar phases to mark specific dates and months in the year. Many civilizations also used the lunar calendar. A birth chart believed to be the oldest with more than 2000 years was discovered in a cave. This shows that people developed an interest in using astrology as an effective tool to unlock knowledge about individuals long ago.

In modern times, birth charts continue to be used to give us a deeper understanding of ourselves and how we relate with others in the world around us. If you are interested in transforming your modern birth chart into a Hellenistic one, it is a good idea to generate your chart using the whole sign system.

First and foremost, you must know your date of birth, year, time, and place before you cast your chart. You can easily interpret your birth chart when you have all the information. However, you must choose a reliable online application to help you get the chart you want. You can get it for free if you carefully look through astrology sites.

When you visit a site like Astrodienst that offers free services to create your chart, click on the create horoscope as a guest user. You need to enter your details, including name, gender, date of birth, time of birth, town, and country where you were born. If you have the time of birth, the entire process becomes much easier.

Under the Ascendant Horoscope chart drawings, click chart drawing and continue. You'll see your accurate and correct sign and all other astrological details below your name. If you want a free one, this is one of the easiest ways of getting it. You will see that the birth chart comes in the form of a wheel, and it should move counter-clockwise starting from the letter ascendant or AC. For instance, if Virgo rules your ascendant or 1st house, the natural planetary ruler is Mercury. This reflects a patient and analytical personality. Mars is the action planet, and it also comes in the first house in Libra. The energy helps create an active vibe.

The second house means your financial issues are in safe hands, and Libra rules the house. Partnerships will improve your finances. As you go through every house, you'll get the interpretation and meaning of every single one.

The Benefits of Mapping Your Astrological Birth Chart

There are many benefits to mapping your astrological birth chart since it helps you know the exact moment you were born. The zodiac is commonly used since it has 12 signs and 12 houses. Each zodiac sign has a different meaning, and each house shows a different aspect of our lives, including family, education, health, love, and work.

The zodiac chart also has the Sun and Moon on top of the ten planets used by astrologers to understand an individual's psyche. If you map out the planet and zodiac signs in a specific astrological house during the time you were born, you can better understand who you are.

The "Thema Mundi" is known as the theme or birth chart of the world since it is one of the oldest methods used to understand different principles in astrology. The Thema Mundi and Hellenistic charts have evolved and are still relevant today. Although the astrological birth or natal chart comprising 12 houses, 12 signs, and 12 planets is commonly used to predict individual life, Hellenistic astrology is still relevant.

Chapter 9: The Hermetic Lots

In this chapter, we will focus on the concept of astrological lots. We will explain how they are believed to be pre-Hellenistic and explore their Hermetic nature. The chapter also explains who Hermes Trismegistus was to astrology. The second part outlines the names and provides instructions for calculating the seven lots. The formulas are based on diurnal and nocturnal charts.

The Hermetic Lots

The Hermetic lots include a set of seven lots. Each lot is linked to one of the seven visible planets, or to the Moon, or the Sun. These lots were attributed to Hermes Trismegistus, who contributed critically to the Hellenistic astrology traditions. The lots can be used to assign topics to houses where the symbolism of the Ascendant and planetary configurations is all crucial to lots. They form a critical component of chart delineation. In the absence of lots, we fail to get the necessary confirmation to gain confidence in what the natal chart indicates.

Background

Lots were mainly used in Hellenistic and medieval astrology, but it is somehow not prioritized in modern astrology. Even today, it seems that astrologers do not use lots regularly. They are mainly misunderstood today due to the marginalization they suffered in European Renaissance astrology. The lots were very popular in ancient astrology.

During the time of William Lilly in the 17th century, the astrologers continued to only use a Lot of Fortune. However, ancient astrologers believe this fortune was used strangely. Lilly's method was known as "Fortuna," which has continued in modern astrology, although it is misunderstood and rarely used. The Lot Fortune remains important since it is used in today's horary practice.

Who Was Hermes Trismegistus in the Tradition of Astrology?

Hermes Trismegistus (thrice-great Hermes) came from the combination of the wisdom gods Thoth and Hermes, and it is regarded as one of the most difficult to understand figures of intellectual history. In Hellenistic Egypt, Thoth was given the name *Hermes*. The "wise Egyptian" has also been associated with magical and mystical writings such as astrology, alchemy, the transcendence of God, and medicine.

Hermes Trismegistus.
See page for author, CC BY 4.0 <https://creativecommons.org/licenses/by/4.0>, via Wikimedia Commons
https://commons.wikimedia.org/wiki/File:Hermes_Trismegistus_illustration_Wellcome_L0016507.jpg

According to the Euhemeristic fashion, Hermes may also be explained as the son of the god. Historians leave the speculation to occultism and alchemy. Hermes Trismegistus is celebrated as the founder of philosophy by the philosophers of the Renaissance, while Freemasons viewed him as their forefather. Hermes is regarded as one of the biggest occult figures and is also associated with the esoteric. His teachings are believed to have influenced the Christian and Muslim versions of religion.

Predicting with Lots

Lots can be used in predictive work, solar returns, planetary years, transits, and places. They also significantly multiplied during the Medieval period due to the growing interest in mundane astrology. Many related to specific weather patterns, political activities, and commodities are used with mundane predictions.

Several lots are mentioned in Hellenistic texts, and their meanings can be confusing since there may be alternative lots with the same meaning. In the Hellenistic period, there were about 12 very popular lots, most of which related to family matters and general issues about life. In Medieval astrology, the lots continued to be used. We will focus on the seven most important lots in this chapter and provide formulas for calculating them.

The lot formula follows a sequence from A to B, meaning the lots move between these points during the day and cover the reverse distance at night. The distance "from A to B" is projected from the Ascendant, meaning this is the diurnal formula used to calculate the lot. The following are the calculations of the common lots.

The Lot of Fortune

Fortune is the most famous lot, and it is also known as the Lot of the Moon. It is renowned for things of a physical nature or circumstances surrounding the body. We calculate Fortune by taking the distance from the sect light where the Sun is above the horizon to the non-sect light referring to the Moon when the Sun is below the horizon. Follow the distance from the Ascendant and observe the degree and the house it lands in.

The formula for Lot of Fortune is:

- **Day Chart:** Ascendant + Moon Sun
- **Night Chart:** Ascendant − Moon + Sun

The sun can be above the horizon, affecting the chart massively. You must reverse the measurement between the moon and the sun at night. When plotting, you'll obtain the arch by measuring from the moon to the sun, using the signs for direction.

Fortune is not only about money and luck. We can better think of it as chance and situation. Fortune is commonly used to signify the things that can befall you outside your control, especially if they relate to health. The Lot of Fortune was used in other quarters to represent fortune, body, and health. Astrologers used a fortune to indicate wealth or material well-being, whereas the horary charts use it to mark success.

However, Fortune alone is not a perfect indicator of health and wealth. It has its place when it comes to delineating each topic. Fortune can be used as a predictive factor concerning occurrences involving finances or the body.

Success or wealth is a complex matter to determine and is based on other factors like fixed stars. Fortune can indicate something that will turn out to be the opposite of the current situation.

The Lot of Spirit

The Lot of Fortune is concerned with the body, well-being, fortune, and health of the person involved. The formula for the Lot of Spirit is the reverse of the one used for the Lot of Fortune. The formulas are as follows:

- **Day Chart:** Ascendant - Moon + Sun
- **Night Chart:** Ascendant + Moon - Sun

The calculation of the Lot of Spirit is opposite to Fortune and distant from the ascendant, which means they complement each other. Connected to creativity and your will—can show how you will act and control yourself when dealing with certain situations.

Just like Fortune, the Spirit has a meaning closely related to the Ascendant, especially the significations of character and capability. The significations are more commonly associated with the house ruler than the place. The spirit figures involved in Hellenistic treatments include temperament, character, and professional aptitude. It also ventures into the analysis of mental and bodily ailments in Valens. Social and mental circumstances are the common denominators to all the significations, although health is not completely overlooked.

The Lot of Necessity

The Lot of Necessity signifies submissions, constraints, struggles, hatreds, enmities, wars, and all other restrictive things that can befall people as a result of their birth. It is also known as the Lot of Poverty, the Lot of Mercury, or the Lot of Small-mindedness.

The following formula represents the Lot:

- **Day Chart:** Ascendant + Fortune – Mercury
- **Night Chart:** Ascendant + Mercury – Fortune

The Lot of Necessity is not very common in Hellenistic astrology, but it is one of the most effective, according to Valens. The opposite of this particular lot is the Lot of Love. The significations of the Lot Necessity are connected to negative associations and are also linked to Mercury. It relates to how one addresses the issue of challengers, competitors, adversaries, and enemies.

When the law is in a good state, it reflects things like the prevailing competition, disputes, and fair treatment of the law. The lot shows attacks from adversaries, legal challenges, unfair treatment, and hatred in its bad state. Love focuses on different types of relationships we pursue, and Necessity relates to the relationships we need to deal with or rather avoid.

The Lot of Eros

The Lot of Eros, Lot of Love, Lot of Desire, or Lot of Venus. It signifies the appetites we have for mutual favor and friendship. Its formula is:

- **Day Chart:** Ascendant + Venus – Spirit
- **Night Chart:** Ascendant + Spirit – Venus

The opposite of the Lot of Love is the Lot of Necessity. These two lots have a special relationship. The significations of Love are connected to those of Venus and the 7th Place. The lot mainly pertains to friendship, desire, and enjoyable associations and alliances. Sympathy between the signs of equal ascension is usually more robust if it is in the charts with sympathetic crosses. Love was used for delineating sexuality, friendship, and what people usually do for pleasure.

The Lot of Courage

The formula for Lot of Courage is represented as follows:

- **Day Chart:** Ascendant + Fortune − Mars
- **Night Chart:** Ascendant + Mars − Fortune

In this lot, courage significantly contributes to boldness, might, treachery, and villainy. This sign is based on Mars and provides traits of fortitude to the natives. It is based on the physical body or fortune as well as the actions of Mars. When this lot is placed in the house, it seems to reflect our worst fears and the things we should face. However, with enough courage, you can overcome some of these challenges regardless of fear. Dealing with different situations in life can be challenging, which is why you must have the nerve to face any situation you may encounter.

The Lot of Victory

The Lot of Victory is based on Jupiter and significantly contributes to trust, good expectations, associations, and contests. Its formula is the following:

- **Day Lot:** Ascendant + Jupiter − Spirit
- **Night Lot:** Ascendant + Spirit − Jupiter

While victory is associated with good things such as rewards, it can sometimes contribute to penalties. The penalty is punishment, and it is something that should not be cherished. Therefore, it is a good idea to use this lot to predict positive things that can turn your life around. When approaching different things, you must have a positive attitude and good expectations in whatever you do.

When you achieve your goals, you must show appreciation and gratitude to enjoy them for a long period. Some people fail to attain their goals because of the general fear of the unknown. If you don't have a formidable plan, you may experience different problems in your journey to obtain the things you want. However, nothing is impossible, and you can use this lot to get inspiration.

The Lot of Nemesis

The Lot of Nemesis is based on Saturn, reflecting the different things most likely to impact the natives. If you want to achieve a certain goal, there are a lot of things that can bring you down. For instance, negative publicity or unfavorable media coverage can be your downfall. The formula for this lot is:

- **Day Chart:** Ascendant + Fortune − Saturn
- **Night Lot:** Ascendant + Saturn − Fortune

This lot can contribute to subterranean fates and ice-cold results like impotence, grief, destruction, exile, and quality of death. The following are some of the inescapable aspects that can affect you. In Aries, elements like impatience or the sword in Taurus.

It is vital to understand your sign and the things that are likely to affect you in your endeavor to achieve different goals. In Gemini, the media, slander, and duplicitous lifestyle are some of the issues you must be wary of. Insecurity, getting lost, and large crowds are the major things you should look out for. Pride and arrogance are some major issues you should be aware of if you belong to Leo.

When it comes to Virgo, jumping to conclusions and lacking faith may be your greatest enemies. In Libra, you should be aware of aspects like separation and divorce. In Scorpio, jealousy, murder, plots, and lack of trust are the major threats you can experience. In Capricorn, neglect and carelessness should not characterize your life if you want positive results.

Lots were used in Hellenistic and Medieval astrology, and each lot is linked to the visible planets. These lots were attributed to Hermes, who significantly contributed to Hellenistic astrology. The main function of lots is to help astrologers assign different topics to houses on the birth chart to help the individuals involved predict different things that can impact their lives. Lots form a crucial aspect of chart delineation. Without lots, we may encounter challenges related to interpreting houses and other components in the birth charts.

Chapter 10: Ancient Hellenistic Techniques

In the previous chapter, we covered the Lots. This one will look at the other six important Hellenistic techniques. These include the rising decan, the lord of nativity, dispositors of nativity, planets/lords in the houses, the application and separation of the moon, and the 12th harmonic. We provide a detailed explanation for each concept to help the readers understand its application.

The Rising Decan

Have you ever thought about why people who belong to the same zodiac sign are different? All individuals with the Sun in Aries are different, and the entire birth chart determines this. Ancient astrologers divided each zodiac sign into divisions known as decans or decanates. The zodiac signs are divided using the method of triplicities, including any three of the four classical elements, namely water, air, fire, and earth. Each zodiac sign is, therefore, subdivided into three equal parts consisting of ten degrees each.

If you want to understand different things taking place in your life, it might be necessary to know these decans. The decans have proven effective, especially in predictive astrology in the horoscope. The ruler of the rising decan in a particular sign on the chart dramatically influences the entire life if the ruler makes any meaningful elements during the time in question. The influence of the decan affects different aspects of the zodiac.

A natal chart has twelve zodiac signs, meaning each sign occupies 30 degrees. The twelve signs constitute 360 degrees to create a complete natal chart. Each sign is subdivided into three decans consisting of 10 degrees. Each decan consists of a ruler that becomes a sub-ruler of that particular sign. When you familiarize yourself with the triplicities, including earth, fire, water, and air, it becomes easier to know the sub-rulers for each particular decan. Each sign's decan belongs to the same triplicity, coming in the same order as in the zodiac. For instance, Aries is the first decan of Aries, and it is ruled by Mars, whereas the second decan is Leo, which is ruled by the Sun. Therefore, the second decan of Aries is also ruled by the Sun. You should know that each decan belonging to the same triplicity, in this case, has a fire element.

The Aries decans as follows:

First Decan Aries: From March 21 to 30th, 0 degrees to 10 degrees and is ruled by Mars. The first decan is the most energetic and influenced by Mars. The people who belong to this decan can excite other people around them and have an endearing childlike innocence. They have great enthusiasm and want to live to the fullest.

Second Decan Aries: From March 31st to April 9th, 10 degrees to 20 degrees and is ruled by the Sun. The second decan consists of rays from the Sun, and the individuals who belong to this decan will maintain their aims, principles, and ambitions even under trying conditions. They are focused, and this helps them focus on the bigger picture.

Third Decan Aries: From April 10th to 20th, 20 degrees to 30 degrees and is ruled by Jupiter. This third decan consists of rays from Jupiter. It is bold, eager, and shows signs of always wanting to be first. The individuals who belong to this decan are intellectuals with a strong sense of individualism. They try hard to avoid scenarios where they are forced to conform to or adopt the herd mentality. They are independent and smart enough not to fall for other people's demands.

The Lord of Nativity

One planet, the Ruler of the Horoscope, or Chart Ruler, is described as the Lord of the Nativity, and this is the Lord of the Ascendant. However, specific rules are used to determine the Lord of the first house. A poorly aspected Lord of the Ascendant in an uncongenial sign can be replaced by a planet that is more elevated if it exists. Other planets should be considered to determine the Lord of the Nativity using the two approaches outlined below:

First Approach

1. If the planet is angular, the Lord becomes the domicile lord of the Midheaven.
2. The planet found in the Midheaven (or 10th House) is the Lord. If there is no planet in the Midheaven, the Lord becomes a planet found in the 11th house.

Second Approach

Other planets can also become Lord of the Nativity when the following conditions exist.

1. The planet is the domicile lord of the Ascendant.
2. The planet within the rising sign with links to the Ascendant.
3. The Lord of the Moon.
4. The Lot of Fortune.
5. If a planet can be in heliacal (the last phase of a planet) - setting, rising, or retrograde within a space of seven days of birth. In the event of multiple planets, the one not under the beams will be the preferred choice.
6. The prenatal lunation can be the bound lord.

The Lord of the Nativity is generally viewed as the plane with the following features.

- Can rise out from the beams of the Sun
- According to the zodiacal rulership, a planet that has more dignity or is more familiar with its location.
- It must be the most powerful depending on its configuration concerning other stars in the chart.
- It should be the most powerful in relation to the nativity figure.

Dispositors of Nativity

The Natal ruler or the Lord of that particular house is the dispositor. The term dispositor means "arranger" in Latin or also refers to the process of setting order. In astrology, a dispositor is known as a planet capable of disposing of another planet. In other words, that planet wields more power or influences the planet because it is found in its house. Dispose also means to arrange or regulate.

When the Lord is placed by a sign found within a particular chart, this shows the sign's influence on the cusp. The placement of the lord by the house within the same chart also shows related areas that control the house's affairs. The Lord of the First house is known as the Lord of the Ascendant. The aspects that exist between the dispositors of the two houses show how the connections in their affairs influence the individual's life.

If the Lord of one house is posited in another, mutual house reception happens. This pairing combines the affairs and shows the links between the two houses involved. The situation is similar to planetary mutual reception, where the energies in the affairs of the two houses are shared.

Planets/Lords in the Houses

The birth chart is more like a snapshot reflecting the connection between the Earth, other planets, and your life. The chart consists of 12 houses, representing where the real action of your life takes place. The date, time, and location of your birth will point to the sign that will rule the house on your chart. The rulership can be attributed to the zodiac signs or the points of a house where they intersect on the wheel.

The house is the grounding force of astrology when it comes to Earthly matters. For instance, each house is associated with different aspects of life like career, love, relationships, and home. Knowing your house will help you gain a deeper understanding of yourself. The houses can also give your insight into different things that might happen to you. If you can predict certain things in your life, you can take corrective measures to prepare for anything.

The zodiac wheel starts with the first house or Ascendant, which represents the position of the Sun where it rose during the time of your birth. The sun governs yourself, your first impression, and your identity. The houses move anti-clockwise around the zodiacal wheel. They encompass broad themes of family, society, and other elements that affect our lives in many ways.

When different planets move around the Sun and the zodiac sign, they pass through the houses. For example, when the planet Venus passes through Aries during the time of your birth, and it is in your first house of individuality, then topics like confidence and self-love will feature prominently in your lifetime. As a result, astrologers make different chart interpretations based on signs, planets, and the houses in your birth chart.

When it comes to the first six houses are known as "personal houses" since they govern various aspects of daily life, family, and community. The last six houses are known as "interpersonal houses" since they control experiences that include relationships, career, travel, and friendships. These components influence our lives in many ways, and they often determine the outcomes of different things we do in life.

For instance, the first house concerns beginnings and dictates the origins of identity and the self, your new endeavors, and outward appearance. The zodiac sign that regulates your chart's first house is the ascendant or the rising sign. Therefore, the first house is significant since it determines how you present yourself to others and how they perceive you. The self in each individual creates first impressions of other people, which are vital since they spell out how you will relate to them. Other houses also define other characteristics that shape you. You must know your house in your natal chart to better understand yourself.

The Application

Ancient Hellenistic techniques were designed in a way that they would help people study different aspects of their lives using celestial objects. If you want to look for insights into your natal chart or daily horoscope, you can use any of the many available astrology apps. For instance, different types of astrology books and other online applications provide a wide range of information about the Earth, stars, and other planets.

There are free options you can get, and these provide details about zodiac-related information that help you better understand yourself. The Moon calendar is another simple version that allows you to track the cycles of the Moon and incorporate its phases into your daily routine. The Moon phases mean different things you can apply in your life. You can also learn different astrological lessons by observing the changes in the world around you.

The 12th Harmonic

The 12th harmonic charts are part of modern astrology since they employ advanced astrological methods. Harmonic astrology consists of a detailed interpretation of different energies broken down from natal aspects to a chart. The 12th harmonic is regarded as the secondary self. The connection of the Duads to the natal shows that the 12th Harmonic is very accurate.

The 12th Harmonic reveals different aspects about people, such as channeling their energies towards certain themes in life like power, creativity, sexuality, or love. The duads are layers of natal planets or the points that modify their energies. The interpretations of the twelfth harmonic readings significantly influence human behavior in many ways.

Apart from the Lots, six Hellenistic astrology techniques are also used for predictive purposes. They help people gain insight into aspects of their lives that are not readily apparent. While some of these techniques are ancient, they are used in other cultures and influence people's lives differently. It is essential to understand each technique before applying it to your life if you want to get meaningful results.

Chapter 11: Make Your Own Astrolabe

In the previous chapters, we discussed different Hellenistic techniques that astrologers used to perform different tasks, including the predictive functions based on celestial features. In this chapter, we will focus on astrolabes which are also fundamental tools for astrologers. We explain how Hellenistic astrologers used them and how the readers can apply the knowledge in their lives. Finally, you will find step-by-step instructions on how to create an astrolabe.

What Is an Astrolabe?

An astrolabe is a scientific tool used for observational purposes, calculating time, or generating the desired results using the universe. It enables astronomers to use the position of the Sun or prominent stars to calculate results that can be used for different purposes like navigation. Astrologers used astrolabes to gain insight into the image of the celestial sphere to help them learn various things about a person's life.

Astrolabes can be traced back to the 6th century and have been widely used since the early Middle Ages in different parts of the world. Around the 15th century, they were adopted by explorers, astrologers, mariners, and others to study celestial spheres. Astrolabes were viewed as the most commonly used astrological tool until the 1650s when more advanced devices were invented.

The astrolabe started as an engraved metal disc, but new features were added over time. Since its invention, there have been different types of astrolabes with smaller and bigger variants. They were used for various purposes, including navigation, calculating time, exploration, calculating horoscopes, astrology, prayer, astronomy, timekeeping, and creating birth charts.

How Hellenistic Astrologers Used Astrolabes

Hellenistic astrologers mainly used this instrument to study different aspects of birth charts. An astrolabe is a disc (Mater) that holds plates (Tympan) and can measure the specific location of the heavenly bodies. Above the tympan and mater is a rete (a "spider's web" in Latin, thus a sort of network) that can freely rotate, consisting of several pointers. These pointers were used to indicate the positions of the brightest stars in the sky.

There are many different shapes of pointers—balls, hands, leaves, stars, and many more. Using stars, you can rotate the pointer until the stars move over the projections. Each rotation denotes a day in the passage of time.

The astronomers assumed that the stars in the sky were positioned at an equal distance from the Earth when they mapped the heavens. Using this model, they created a two-dimensional representation of the celestial sphere – visible on astrolabes and star charts. The result produced a starry representation of a map on Earth. The front part of the astrolabe was used to show the map of the night sky that appeared in the form of a rotating net-like rete. Medieval writers described the rete as the spider.

The most crucial component of the traditional astrolabe is a circular metal plate with a diameter of about 6 inches. It can hang in a vertical position when suspended by a ring. The other side of the disc is black, consisting of several circle measurements like 360 degrees, 12 for months, 365 ¼ for days in a year, and others. The engravings were used for trigonometric calculations, and the outer circle on the astrolabe had 24 divisions representing the hours. Zodiacal constellations were used to create a calendar. The equator and tropics were carved in the center of the disc consisting of a celestial pole.

Another disc could be affixed to the front of the instrument and rotated. Several holes were made into the disc to allow the user to see through the body of the astrolabe. The cuts were explicitly meant for creating a map of the sky. They also included a broad annulus, flames, and tongues pointing to major stars in the sky. Thin engraved papers or discs were also used between the outer circle and the sky disc.

The astrolabe and its components were mainly used to measure distance and time by using the shadow cast by the alidade, also known as a gnomon. The gnomon produces a shadow from a conical-shaped feature on the circular disk's edge. This led to the formation of an angle equal to the difference between the altitude and time for that specific time of the day. The angle could be used to tell the difference in times of the day, so it helps the astrologers create a birth chart and mark dates. If one wanted to use the astrolabe to measure altitude, one had to determine the latitude first.

There were spikes on the rete that corresponded with the star positions. We can look to the dog's head as the position of the Dog Star (Sirius). It could also show the elliptical path of the sun concerning a star and how it moved through the zodiac signs.

Another critical aspect of the rete is that it consisted of a plate written with the projection of the sky above the observer at a specific latitude. This plate could be removed, and calibrated pieces are placed to measure different latitudes. The rotating rule fixed on the center of the astrolabe was mainly used for readings.

The astrolabe has a rotating bar at its back called the label or alidade, and it is used to measure the altitude of different elements above the horizon of various celestial bodies. The back part of the instrument consists of degrees that were used for taking measurements of the altitude. It is also engraved with zodiac signs and a calendar. The astrologers used these features to measure the positions of different objects in the sky.

Users can use data from the astrolabe to determine their position in time and space. This information played a critical role in astrology since it was used to determine answers to several questions about celestial issues. The data was also used as an inference to solve different problems encountered by people in their lives.

Astronomy has greatly influenced astrology as the measurements of the planets and stars has become more exact. The movement of these heavenly bodies can also be tracked more accurately. Astrolabes have been invaluable and have become more accurate across the ages.

Astrolabes were later adopted in different parts of the world, and they shaped the subject of astrology as we know it today. Although astrolabes are rarely used today, they are still quite accurate. You can make your instrument if you want to have a feel of how ancient astrologers conducted their work.

Conclusion

Since the beginning of time, we've been observing the sky, planets, and stars. Every civilization, along with its culture and traditions, was essentially brought to life when a group of people tried to make sense of the world in their own way. There is no better way to learn about the world than by seeking answers from the world itself, hence, the development of the study of astrology. Records of astrological practices date back to 30,000 to 10,000 B.C.E, meaning that our modern-day understanding of the field was shaped over eons.

At first, people used to view astrology in a deterministic light; they believed that natural laws encompass astrology influenced personal will, fate, living environment, etc. And these beliefs made sense because it was easier for them to align their lives to the Earth's natural cycles, considering their hunting-gathering, agricultural, and nomadic lifestyles.

The distinct studies of astronomy and astrology were regarded as the same field for several centuries. Besides the lack of modern-day technology and limited resources of the time, people believed that both areas of practice went hand-in-hand because of their superstitious beliefs. Eras ago, people's ability to survive depended on the general condition of nature. Many cultures thought that if the Gods were angry, they'd hold out on the rainfall to cause drought or instigate a flood to wipe out the crops. To prepare for the unknown, humans tried to deduce patterns by keeping track of the stars.

Humanity and technology evolved, and so did astrology. We've expanded our knowledge and elevated our consciousness throughout the centuries. The advancements we've made in fields like astronomy, science, mathematics, and technology have made it possible for us to have more control over our lives. Instead of needing astrology to survive and resorting to it from a place of fear, we now view it as a tool. Modern-day astrology is not only thought of as a way to enhance one's life (by learning how to use it to increase self-awareness, plan, improve relationships, etc.) but also as a means of entertainment by many.

Now that you've read this book, you know how astrology has evolved over the centuries to take the form we know today and have a great starting point if you wish to learn the ins and outs of astrology. It is also an ideal source of extensive knowledge for more experienced readers who wish to learn more. Either way, reading this book has given you a lot of insight into where many modern-day astrological practices and doctrines originate.

Bonus: Glossary of Astrological Terms

1. **Ascendant** - also referred to as the rising sign - is present on the cusp of the 1st house on a natal chart. It rises on the eastern horizon at the time of a person's birth.
2. **Astrological Compendium** - an astrological instrument used to tell the time and to perform various calculations. This contraption consists of a number of devices, including a sundial, a compass, lunar and solar volvelles, and a perpetual calendar.
3. **Benefic** - planets on your birth chart that have a positive or good influence on your life, and are said to bring fortune.
4. **Besiegement** - the placement of a planet between two malefic planets or their aspect points. Contrastingly, it can also be the placement of a planet between two benefic planets.
5. **Celestial bodies** - used to define objects in space, mainly planets (Mars, Jupiter, Saturn, Neptune, etc.), the Moon, or stars like the Sun.
6. **Constellations** - a group of stars forming recognizable patterns named after mythological figures.
7. **Culmination** - the transit of a celestial object across the meridian. Also known as meridian transits, these paths are circular in nature, and appear to be occurring because of the Earth's rotation.

8. **Cusp** – the natal chart consists of a total of 12 houses and 12 signs. The line that divides these signs or houses is referred to as the cusp. For instance, if your birth placement is on the cusp of Scorpio and Sagittarius, that means that the Sun was placed over this dividing line when you were born.
9. **Decan** – subdivisions of every zodiac sign to further narrow down personality traits and astrological information. Each zodiac sign is divided into three decans, each one being 10 degrees. Each of these decans also have planetary rulers, which makes them sub-rulers that give information about a specific persona.
10. **Descendant** – the opposite point of the ascendant, and also the point where the ecliptic sets. Mostly marks the end of the seventh house, and is one of the four points marking the natal chart.
11. **Delineation** – the interpretation of an astrological natal or birth chart. An astrologer usually does these, but it can also be computer generated these days.
12. **Depressed** – a planet is said to be depressed or in fall when it's in the zodiac exactly opposite to the one it rules. This essentially means that the ruling planet's influences block the planet's expression and general characteristics. Matters associated with this planet will likely bring you distress, worry, and a lack of appreciation.
13. **Eclipse** – when the Moon's orbit aligns with the Sun to create a lunation effect, it is known as an eclipse. Different types of eclipses take place, primarily lunar and solar eclipses. These occurrences are said to activate the lunar nodes, which can have a dramatic effect on our zodiacs. Depending on when these eclipses take place, they can majorly affect the aspects associated with the specific zodiac signs and bring considerable changes in your life.
14. **Equinox** – an equinox takes place when the Earth aligns its orbit directly around the sun. The Sun is thus positioned directly above the equator, resulting in the night and day being equal in length, i.e., 12 hours. This occurrence only occurs twice a year, namely on the 20th of March, known as the spring equinox, and the 23rd of September, the autumnal equinox.
15. **Exalted** – a planet is said to be exalted (or in domicile) when it is in the zodiac sign that it rules. It feels at home in its territory, and is thus comfortable expressing traits, and characteristics specific to

the planet. Matters associated with this planet will bring you recognition and appreciation.

16. **Heliacal rising is** said to occur when the Sun moves so ahead of the star that the star becomes visible before the Sun rises in the morning. So, a heliacal rising will result in the star rising way before the Sun does every morning, and is visible until its light overwhelms it.

17. **Heliacal setting** – It is the opposite of heliacal rising. It takes place when the star sets after the sunset. This is when the Sun is far below the western horizon that it becomes briefly visible in the evening.

18. **Hermeticism** – hermetic thought is associated with the deity Hermes. According to this school of thought in astrology, the planet's movements are considered to have meaning beyond their physical sense and actually have metaphorical value. In this sense, these movements directly affect our lives in the sense that it doesn't dictate our actions, but it does influence our decisions.

19. **Horoscope** – A horoscope is another name for a natal chart and is used to describe an astrological chart representing the various positions of the luminaries, i.e., the Sun and the Moon, as well as the twelve planets at the time of an event. These positions are said to greatly influence said event.

20. **Latitude** – latitudes are used to describe the specific location with reference to the equator. Specifically, terrestrial latitude is used to define the angular distance of a location from north or south of the terrestrial equator. Similarly, the celestial latitude is defined as the angular distance of a certain location from the south or north of the ecliptic.

21. **Longitude** – longitude goes hand in hand with latitude numerics to describe specific locations with reference to the equator. Namely, terrestrial longitudes are used to define the angular distance of a location east or west of the meridian, whereas celestial longitude defines the angular distance from a point along the ecliptic.

22. **Luminary body** – luminaries are used to describe celestial bodies that produce illumination and are considered the most important astronomical bodies. Luminaries translate to light sources; two primary luminary bodies include the sun, and the Moon. Stars are also considered to be important luminary bodies.

23. **Lunar cycle** – the lunar cycle follows the Moon's transit around the Earth's orbit. This movement around the Earth and the Sun creates a shadow on the Moon's far side, limiting the light that is reflected back to Earth. This results in the formation of specific shapes of the Moon. These shapes result in the moon's eight phases, including new Moon, waxing crescent, 1st quarter, waxing gibbous, full Moon, waning gibbous, 3rd quarter, and waning crescent. Each of these phases has its own meaning and affects the zodiacs.
24. **Malefic** – according to astrology, a malefic planet is said to bring misfortune and back luck to people born under it. Usually, Mars and Saturn are considered malefic planets, with Mars being the lesser between the two, and Saturn being the greater harbinger of bad luck.
25. **Meridian** - is the circle passing through the north and south of the horizon from a place of observation.
26. **Meridian distance** - is the distance of a planet or a celestial body from the meridian, and is measured in degrees, starting from right ascension to the celestial equator.
27. **Midheaven** – one of the four points on a natal chart, the midheaven point intersects the meridian vertically and is located on the upper end of this intersecting line.
28. **Planets** – celestial objects or heavenly bodies moving along fixed orbits on the axis of fixed stars, mainly, the Sun and the Moon. These include Mars, Venus, Jupiter, Saturn, Neptune, and Pluto.
29. **Prenatal lunation** – prenatal lunation charts are used to gain insight about our interactions in this world. These are for both new and full moons, and highlight our specific capabilities and characteristics.
30. **Retrograde** – planets are said to be in retrograde when they look like they start moving backwards, or in the opposite direction of their primary movement. This takes place among the five non-luminary planets and significantly affects zodiacs.
31. **Rising time is** the time required by a zodiac sign to rise over the horizon from a specific place of observation.
32. **Ruling planet** – ruling planets oversee various zodiac signs, and thus influence how a certain sign will interact. The ruling planet of

a zodiac sign gives insight into a person's primary traits and personalities.

33. **Solstice** – the opposite of an equinox, a solstice takes place when the Sun reaches its most southward or northward excursion. Every year, two solstices take place, around 21st June (Summer Solstice) and 21st December (Winter Solstice).

34. **Triplicity** – triplicities are sub classifications of zodiac groups into a group 3 forming an equilateral triangle. These triplicities are thus ruled by three planets, primary, secondary, and participating rulers.

35. **Wicca** – Wiccan religion is classified as a modern Pagan religion. Experts categorize this school of thought as both a newly developed religious movement and as part of the esoteric religions.

36. **Ziggurat** – a structure, usually found in ancient Mesopotamia. It has a terraced structure of receding steps. This was most commonly utilized for viewing stars and other celestial bodies.

37. **Zodiac** – a total of twelve zodiacs originate from various constellations visible in the sky.

Here's another book by Mari Silva that you might like

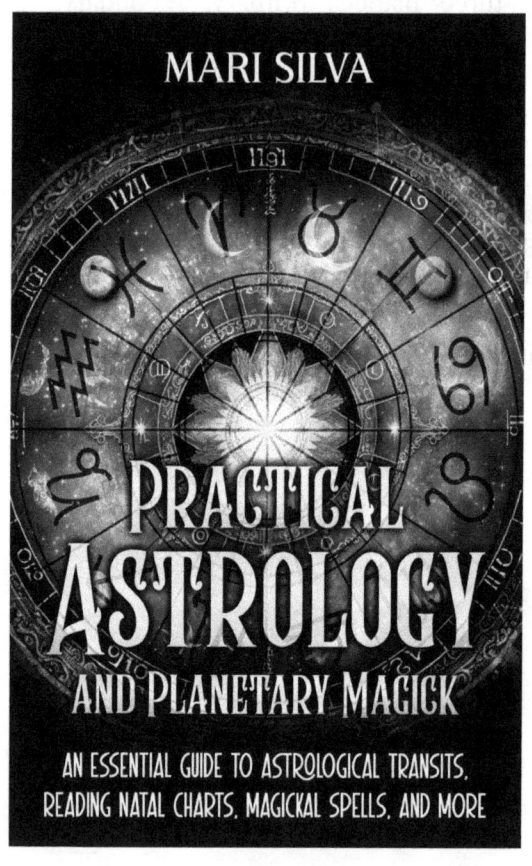

Your Free Gift
(only available for a limited time)

Thanks for getting this book! If you want to learn more about various spirituality topics, then join Mari Silva's community and get a free guided meditation MP3 for awakening your third eye. This guided meditation mp3 is designed to open and strengthen ones third eye so you can experience a higher state of consciousness. Simply visit the link below the image to get started.

https://spiritualityspot.com/meditation

References

geomancy | method of divination. (n.d.). In Encyclopedia Britannica.

Geomancy - fortune-telling. (n.d.). Magizzle.Com. https://www.magizzle.com/geomancy/

Painter, S. (n.d.). Geomancy in Feng Shui for beginners. LoveToKnow. https://feng-shui.lovetoknow.com/feng-shui-tips/geomancy-feng-shui-beginners

(N.d.-a). Princeton.Edu. https://www.princeton.edu/~ezb/geomancy/geostep.html

(N.d.-b). Princeton.Edu. https://www.princeton.edu/~ezb/geomancy/geostep.html#:~:text=The%20astrological%20method%20(which%20is,the%20use%20of%20an%20astrolabe.

(N.d.-c). Psychicscience.Org. https://psychicscience.org/geomancy

(N.d.). Mapsofindia.Com. https://www.mapsofindia.com/my-india/uncategorized/significance-of-astrology-in-our-lives#:~:text=It%20is%20an%20importance%20aspect,mishap%20related%20to%20planetary%20positions

Astrology: Ancient and modern. (n.d.). Classicsforall.Org.Uk. https://classicsforall.org.uk/reading-room/ad-familiares/astrology-ancient-and-modern

Cap, A. (2018, March 20). Why learn ancient astrology and its history? - Anthony cap. Medium. https://medium.com/@sevenstarsastrology/why-learn-ancient-astrology-and-its-history-b533c8d1c9e

Experience, N. S. L., & Marchesella, J. (2021, April 30). The benefits of astrology. Thriveglobal.Com. https://thriveglobal.com/stories/the-benefits-of-astrology/

Guest Column. (n.d.). 5 reasons to study astrology and how it can help your personal growth. Smudailycampus.Com.

https://www.smudailycampus.com/sponsoredcontent/tactadv/5-reasons-to-study-astrology-and-how-it-can-help-your-personal-growth

Hammonds, O. (2014, August 5). 3 benefits of astrology. 3 Benefits Of. https://www.3benefitsof.com/3-benefits-of-astrology/

Macmillan, P. (2022, June 1). Why is astrology making a twenty-first-century comeback? Pan Macmillan. https://www.panmacmillan.com/blogs/lifestyle-wellbeing/the-popularity-of-astrology

Obert, C. (2011, October 12). Traditional and modern astrology. Student of Astrology. https://studentofastrology.com/2011/10/traditional-and-modern-astrology/

October. (2020, October 27). The three major forms of modern-day astrology. Brewminate: A Bold Blend of News and Ideas. https://brewminate.com/the-three-major-forms-of-modern-day-astrology/

Rubedo Press. (2019, January 5). The first five steps in learning traditional astrology. Rubedo Press. https://rubedo.press/propaganda/2018/12/21/first-five-steps

Schatsky, B. (2020, June 18). Astrology is a 21st-century trend. The Daily Northwestern. https://dailynorthwestern.com/2020/06/17/campus/astrology-an-unexpected-and-uniquely-modern-anchor-during-times-of-crisis/

Smallwood, C. (2019, October 17). Astrology in the age of uncertainty. New Yorker (New York, N.Y.: 1925). https://www.newyorker.com/magazine/2019/10/28/astrology-in-the-age-of-uncertainty

What are the differences between traditional and modern astrology? (n.d.). Quora. https://www.quora.com/What-are-the-differences-between-traditional-and-modern-astrology

About the name wandering stars — ☿ wandering stars. (n.d.). ☿ Wandering Stars. https://www.wandering-stars.net/about-the-name-wandering-stars

Adams, M. S. (2021, May 10). Mercury, the moon, and the great word. Interlochen Public Radio. https://www.interlochenpublicradio.org/2021-05-10/mercury-the-moon-and-the-great-word

All about mercury. (n.d.). Nasa.Gov. https://spaceplace.nasa.gov/all-about-mercury/en/

Amun. (n.d.). Egyptianmuseum.Org. https://egyptianmuseum.org/deities-amun

Ask-Aladdin. (n.d.). Isis Egyptian god - Isis the goddess of fertility - AskAladdin. Egypt Travel Experts. https://ask-aladdin.com/egypt-gods/isis/

AstroTwins. (2020, March 2). What are Benefic and Malefic Planets in Astrology? Astrostyle: Astrology and Daily, Weekly, Monthly Horoscopes by The AstroTwins. https://astrostyle.com/benefic-and-malefic-planets/

Beringer, B. (2021, August 26). Your Jupiter sign can tell you A lot about your personal growth. Bustle. https://www.bustle.com/life/jupiter-sign-meaning-astrology

Beringer-Tobing, B. (2022, March 24). What your Saturn sign means in astrology. POPSUGAR. https://www.popsugar.com/smart-living/saturn-sign-meaning-48757756

Bisht, N. (2022, March 31). Venus & Astrology: How the planet of love affects your love life. The Hindustan Times. https://www.hindustantimes.com/astrology/horoscope/venus-astrology-how-the-planet-of-love-affects-your-love-life-101648629708393.html

Brown, M. (2021, October 28). What your Mars sign means about your energy, anger, and sex life. Shape. https://www.shape.com/lifestyle/mind-and-body/astrology/mars-sign-meaning

Bunch, E. (2020, April 16). This is what it means when you have an exalted planet in your astrology chart. Well+Good. https://www.wellandgood.com/exalted-planet-astrology/

Cain, F. (2008, May 15). How Did Venus Get its Name? Universe Today. https://www.universetoday.com/14281/how-did-venus-get-its-name/

Cessna, A. (2009, July 8). Names of the planets. Universe Today. https://www.universetoday.com/34362/names-of-the-planets/

Coffey, J. (2008, June 4). Mars is Named After. Universe Today. https://www.universetoday.com/14825/mars-is-named-after/

Cradle of civilization. (2016, December 24). Cradle of Civilization. https://aratta.wordpress.com/2016/12/24/the-mythological-origin-of-mercury/

Crane, L. (2016, April 4). Wandering stars: A brief history of defining 'planet' –. Lateral Magazine.

Davies, W. (Originally published: March 22, 2018). Mercury is entering retrograde again. This is why so many people care. Time. https://time.com/5207161/mercury-retrograde-astrology-history/

Deimos, moon of Mars – the Solar System on sea and sky. (n.d.). Seasky.Org. http://www.seasky.org/solar-system/mars-deimos.html

Dhankher, N. (2021, September 12). Jupiter's Retrograde Transit In Capricorn 2021: How to tap into its abundance. The Hindustan Times. https://www.hindustantimes.com/astrology/your-fortune-today/jupiters-retrograde-transit-in-capricorn-2021-how-to-tap-into-its-abundance-101631343877265.html

Early Times. (n.d.). Nasa.Gov. https://mars.nasa.gov/allaboutmars/mystique/history/early/

Editors, C. R. (2018). Thoth: The history and legacy of the ancient Egyptian god who maintains the universe. Createspace Independent Publishing Platform.

ESO. (n.d.). ESO https://www.eso.org/public/outreach/eduoff/vt-2004/Background/Infol2/EIS-D9.html

Exalted and debilitated planets. (2016, February 20). AstrologerPanditJi.Com. https://www.astrologerpanditji.com/page25.htm

Francos, E. (2022, January 19). What does your Saturn sign mean in astrology? YourTango. https://www.yourtango.com/2019328839/astrology-saturn-natal-chart-meaning-each-zodiac-sign-house

Grossman, L. (2016). What if... we put a colony on Mars? New Scientist (1971), 232(3100), 38. https://doi.org/10.1016/s0262-4079(16)32131-5

Hall, M. (2007, April 8). Mercury in Astrology. LiveAbout. https://www.liveabout.com/mercury-in-astrology-206363

How did Mars and its moons get their names? (n.d.). Cool Cosmos. https://coolcosmos.ipac.caltech.edu/ask/86-How-did-Mars-and-its-moons-get-their-names-

How did Mercury get its name? (n.d.). Cool Cosmos. https://coolcosmos.ipac.caltech.edu/ask/33-How-did-Mercury-get-its-name-

How did Saturn get its name? (n.d.). Cool Cosmos. https://coolcosmos.ipac.caltech.edu/ask/115-How-did-Saturn-get-its-name-

How did the planets get their names? (n.d.). Cool Cosmos. https://coolcosmos.ipac.caltech.edu/ask/196-How-did-the-planets-get-their-names-

How did Venus get its name? (n.d.). Cool Cosmos. https://coolcosmos.ipac.caltech.edu/ask/41-How-did-Venus-get-its-name-

What is Jupiter? https://www.nasa.gov/audience/forstudents/5-8/features/nasa-knows/what-is-jupiter-58.html

In Depth. (n.d.-a). NASA Solar System Exploration. https://solarsystem.nasa.gov/planets/venus/in-depth/

In Depth. (n.d.-b). NASA Solar System Exploration. https://solarsystem.nasa.gov/planets/saturn/in-depth/

Interesting facts about Venus. (n.d.). Rmg.Co.Uk https://www.rmg.co.uk/stories/topics/interesting-facts-about-venus

Jawer, J. (2018, January 6). Exalted planets in astrology. Tarot.Com. https://www.tarot.com/astrology/exalted-planets

Jupiter – the generous planet of wealth and wisdom. (2021, October 6). GaneshaSpeaks. https://www.ganeshaspeaks.com/astrology/planets/jupiter/

Jupiter, king of the gods, in Astrology/zodiac. (2015, April 13). Cafeastrology.Com; Cafe Astrology .com. https://cafeastrology.com/jupiter.html

Kedziora-Chudczer, L. (2019, September 9). Curious Kids: why does Saturn have rings? The Conversation. http://theconversation.com/curious-kids-why-does-saturn-have-rings-121433

Kelly, A. (2018, July 31). What the position of Venus in your birth chart means for you. Allure. https://www.allure.com/story/venus-birth-chart-planet-of-love

Machholz, D., Whitt, K. K., & Byrd, D. (2021, November 28). Why is Venus so bright? EarthSky | Updates on Your Cosmos and World; EarthSky. https://earthsky.org/astronomy-essentials/why-is-venus-so-bright/

Mark, J. J. (2017). Nergal. World History Encyclopedia. https://www.worldhistory.org/Nergal/

Mars, god of war, in Astrology/zodiac. (2015a, April 13). Cafeastrology.Com; Cafe Astrology .com. https://cafeastrology.com/mars.html

Mars, god of war, in Astrology/zodiac. (2015b, April 13). Cafeastrology.Com; Cafe Astrology .com. https://cafeastrology.com/mars.html

Mercury, messenger of the gods, in Astrology/zodiac. (2015a, April 19). Cafeastrology.Com; Cafe Astrology .com. https://cafeastrology.com/mercury.html

Mercury, messenger of the gods, in Astrology/zodiac. (2015b, April 19). Cafeastrology.Com; Cafe Astrology .com. https://cafeastrology.com/mercury.html

Oomen, M. (2022, March 15). Find the Benefic and Malefic Planets in Birth chart. Astrology Articles | Clickastro Blog. https://www.clickastro.com/blog/planets-in-birth-chart/

Pappas, S. (2012, June 5). Five odd facts you might not know about Venus. NBC News. https://www.nbcnews.com/id/wbna47694036

Phobos, moon of Mars – the solar system on sea and sky. (n.d.). Seasky.Org. http://www.seasky.org/solar-system/mars-phobos.html

Planet Mercury. (n.d.). Urban Astrologer https://www.urban-astrologer.com/planet-mercury.html

Planet Mercury In Astrology. (n.d.). Astrosage.Com. https://www.astrosage.com/planet/mercury/

Planets & astrology: Saturn. (2016, November 8). Astrostyle: Astrology and Daily, Weekly, Monthly Horoscopes by The AstroTwins; The AstroTwins. https://astrostyle.com/astrology-planets-saturn/

Retrogrades: When planets go "backward" in astrology. (2013, October 19). Astrostyle: Astrology and Daily, Weekly, Monthly Horoscopes by The AstroTwins; The AstroTwins. https://astrostyle.com/learn-astrology/retrogrades/

Saturn. (n.d.). NASA Solar System Exploration. https://solarsystem.nasa.gov/planets/saturn/overview/

Saturn. (2017, February 23). Greek Gods & Goddesses. https://greekgodsandgoddesses.net/gods/saturn/

Saturn in Astrology, zodiac. (2015, April 19). Cafeastrology.Com; Cafe Astrology.com. https://cafeastrology.com/saturn.html

Saturn: Jewel of the solar system. (n.d.). Exploratorium.Edu. https://www.exploratorium.edu/saturn/saturn.html

Sesay, A. (2020, October 20). Your Saturn sign is your cosmic teacher—here's how to find yours. Cosmopolitan. https://www.cosmopolitan.com/lifestyle/a34426595/saturn-sign-meaning/

Stardust, L. (2021, June 11). The best way to get through Mercury retrograde is to do nothing at all. Oprah Daily. https://www.oprahdaily.com/entertainment/a36593904/what-is-mercury-retrograde-meaning-astrology/

Student video: Mars in a minute: Is mars really red? (2020, December 24). Nasa.Gov. https://www.jpl.nasa.gov/edu/learn/video/mars-in-a-minute-is-mars-really-red/

Thomas, K. (2021a, October 22). Here's what a retrograde in astrology means and how it affects you. New York Post. https://nypost.com/article/retrograde-meaning-explained/

Thomas, K. (2021b, December 24). What your Jupiter sign means in astrology and what it reveals about you. New York Post. https://nypost.com/article/jupiter-sign-meaning/

Venus. (n.d.). NASA Solar System Exploration. https://solarsystem.nasa.gov/planets/venus/overview/

Venus astrology symbol – characteristics, planet energy and more. (2018, January 22). Labyrinthos. https://labyrinthos.co/blogs/astrology-horoscope-zodiac-signs/venus-astrology-symbol-characteristics-planet-energy

Ward, K. (2020, April 7). How to find your Mercury sign, AKA the chatty part of your birth chart. Cosmopolitan. https://www.cosmopolitan.com/lifestyle/a32055636/what-is-mercury-sign/

www.ingramcontent.com/pod-product-compliance
Lightning Source LLC
Chambersburg PA
CBHW051853160426
43209CB00006B/1283